BORN WHOLE

Heal your pre-birth trauma

Guide and protect your baby from conception to birth

Wes Gietz

2019

Print ISBN: 978-1-9991214-1-9

Digital ISBN: 978-1-9991214-0-2

FIRST EDITION

www.windwalker.ca

For all the people
born and yet to be born
that they may heal their wounds
and realize their magnificence.

Table of Contents

PART 1

SETTING THE STAGE

Preface

This book is about how we and our children can be born whole.

It is my story, and it is a story that belongs to us all.

This book will stretch your understanding of what is real and what is possible. You may also find that this story feels familiar deep within you, at a level beyond memory or intellect.

As you read, you will learn new information about life before we were born into this beautiful, if not always pretty, world. I invite you to explore the origins of your emotional wounds and limiting beliefs. And as you do so, you will learn new opportunities and techniques for retroactively healing the hurts that are inevitable as we grow in the womb. You will learn how parents can proactively protect their babies from these hurts by accompanying them all the way to birth, providing guidance, protection, reassurance, and love on the way.

I hope that you will come to believe in the healing that can happen before birth and understand how to accomplish that healing. I hope, too, that you will come to appreciate the potential of this healing in your own life and the lives of your children.

What This Book Offers

Humanity needs a new story. We need a story of hope, optimism, and confidence. We need to know that we can be better than we have been.

This book provides a model for part of that new story. In a sense, it is a how-to book about how to heal ourselves and protect our children. One part contains ideas and techniques to help us be healthier in our adult lives. The second shows us how we can bring into this world children who are loved, guided, and healthy from the beginning of their existence.

In this book you will learn how to engage with your pre-birth experiences, discover it is possible to recall and face pre-birth traumas, and learn to heal those traumas. You will learn that healing can reveal the magnificence of these experiences that initially appear filled with pain but are actually full of the beauty and possibilities of being human. You will learn how this can be done by almost anyone, with guidance or unaided.

For the parents or soon-to-be parents, you will also learn how you can be with your own yet-to-be-born (or yet-to-be-conceived!) baby through conception and gestation, providing your presence, love, and compassionate reassurance to that baby on the beautiful journey into this world.

You will be invited to find compassion and admiration for all babies and all mothers, regardless of your gender or identification.

I hope that you will feel encouraged and empowered to explore and pursue your own healing in this phase of life that is so beautiful, so powerful, and so vulnerable.

I anticipate that you will find yourself in awe of the strength of the life force that exists within us all.

The Structure of This Book

After the preface, *part 1* also includes the *introduction*. The *introduction* tells how my life prepared me for the work described here and how I became involved in a research project that created and blazed new trails in the field of prenatal experience and healing.

Part 2: Three Universal Developmental Events explores three of the most significant developmental events that occur before we are born. These events are conception, implantation in the wall of the womb, and the first contraction of labor. They occur in similar fashion for every baby, and the emotional impacts are likely to be similar as well.

The first chapter of *part 3: The Environment of the Womb* is a discussion of two interwoven topics. The first is compelling evidence that every human life is a combination of eternal soul and mortal human being. The second is the uncertain nature of survival during the earliest months of life. This chapter also discusses how these ideas are related.

The second chapter of *part 3* is the story of my personal experience in the emotional, physical, mental, and spiritual environment of my mother's womb. Every mother is unique, and every baby's experience of the womb is consequently also unique.

The last chapter of *part 3* is a discussion of meridian healing techniques. It discusses Emotional Freedom Techniques (EFT), the method I used for healing my own emotional issues during the research.

Part 4: A Bright and Beautiful Future presents the exciting possibility that parents can accompany and guide their own children through life before birth.

The Backdrop: My Beliefs

As you reflect on what you read, I hope you will see how you can use what is offered in this book. Some of this may seem strange, even unbelievable, but all of it is what I have experienced.

I grew up in a strongly religious environment. Perhaps the greatest gift from that early experience was that I understood the concept of spiritual beings. In my Christian family, these were presented as God, the Holy Spirit, and angels. I recall being entranced and mystified by stories in the Bible that were very different from my everyday experience: burning bushes that were not consumed, haloes of light appearing around people as they experienced the Holy Spirit, angels announcing the birth of Jesus, and the resurrection. These were magical events, and they seemed impossible in the modern world.

Later in life, I sought training in shamanic philosophy and techniques. It was on this path that I began to have personal experience of the power described in the biblical stories. It is not necessary for you to believe the same in order to appreciate and apply what you will find here. If my beliefs are outside your understanding of the world, take what works for you and leave the rest. The need for healing is more pressing in this world than the need to agree on philosophical details.

I have found several principles to be true through my studies and my personal experience:

- We are capable of entering altered states of consciousness through deep meditation or hypnosis. In these states we can perceive, communicate, and move unhampered by the limitations of three-dimensional physical reality. For example, we can move our consciousness to other physical locations and see our surroundings there with spiritual vision. You may have heard this referred to as remote viewing or clairvoyance.
- We can communicate spiritually or energetically with other physical beings, both human and nonhuman. We can do this close by or at great distances.
- In deep meditation, we can enter nonphysical dimensions and interact with entities or spirits who do not have physical bodies.
- Angels surround us. I call them angels because the beings I have met in other dimensions or

realities are fundamentally loving. They are actively interested in our well-being. We can communicate directly with these nonphysical entities.

- We can use nonphysical energy for healing. We can do this by ourselves or in concert with spiritual beings.
- As humans, each of us is a melding of a soul and a human body/ego. Our souls incarnate many times. When we incarnate, we choose our lives, our companions, and our circumstances. Within the framework of these "start-up" choices, we have free will.
- Life is to be lived with joy and purpose. For many of us, this will not be easy because of the lives we chose for ourselves as we prepared to incarnate.

The relevance and implications of these experiences, abilities, and understandings will be explored as we go through the narrative and lessons of this book.

Introduction

A New Need, a New Opportunity

We live in a world that is fascinated with technology. We appreciate the benefits of our accomplishments in electronics, communications, travel, entertainment, medicine, and many other areas. At the same time, and even more importantly for our future, we are advancing in our understanding of our emotional nature, our spiritual aspect, and our relationships. We are continuously developing our awareness of both ancient and new ways to learn, heal, and grow.

Today, there is a wide range of energetic and spiritual techniques available to heal physical trauma, negative beliefs, and emotional issues. These techniques can reach into and heal the pain of almost every moment of our lives, whether the painful times are from today or from our earliest years. We can also revisit and heal trauma from past lives or pain carried from our ancestors. Through deep meditation or hypnotherapy, we are able to identify and heal issues and wounds that have lodged in our bodies and hearts from yesterday and from generations ago.

But there is a vitally important segment of our lives that has remained almost out of reach for healing, and that has only recently been recognized as important. That is *the time before we were born*, beginning with the creation of egg and sperm cells; the time of conception, implantation and gestation; and up to the time of labor and birth.

In studies of emotional and psychological health, researchers have found clear evidence that babies are profoundly affected by their experiences in the womb, and that the effects of these experiences remain after birth.[1]

Why have we not given more attention to this important time?

I see two reasons.

First, Western society has believed that stresses or traumas we encounter before birth have no lasting effect. Fortunately, this belief is dissipating. Sophisticated techniques for observing babies in the womb have shown that they are affected by what happens *to* them and *around* them. These effects can be both positive and negative. Among healers, there are many stories of adult clients who can recall pre-birth trauma. Even more significantly, healing prenatal trauma results in definite improvements in the current lives of the clients. I have seen this in my own practice.

Second, it can be a challenge to recognize and address trauma that occurs before birth. Can we know what the yet-to-be-born baby is aware of? If it is aware of itself and its environment, how do we achieve healing when needed?

This book provides answers to these questions.

A Unique and Universal Story

The foundation of this book is the story of my journey from conception to birth. It is the story of a wonderful adventure in becoming.

This journey is one we all have taken, and therefore, this is also the story of every one of us. We have all experienced the marvels and the stresses of conception, implantation in the wall of our mother's womb, gestation, and birth.

Even though the story belongs to all, it is unique for each. My mother's experience included love, joy, worry, work, movement, food, and the other emotional and physical aspects of life. In many respects, her life during this time (and mine while I was in her womb) will have much in common with the life of your mother (and you). So while our individual lives in the womb are as unique to each of us as were the lives of our mothers, you will probably find echoes of my story in your experience.

It has taken me twenty years to understand that this story deserves to be told. I needed to appreciate how powerful this healing was for me, and I needed to understand its impact on my life. The experiences described here have enriched my life immensely, and I realized it could enrich others' lives too. I comprehend in a new way what a miracle it is to be born, what a miracle it is simply to exist. I see how strong and resilient human life is. I know from direct experience how liberating it is to experience the healing of emotional wounds and limiting beliefs that were embedded in my being before I was born.

Through exploring my personal narrative, I also found deeper and more universal implications in the story. Those deeper meanings are what make this book important.

First, when we heal the issues, challenges, and traumas of the time before we are born, we become healthier and more complete *now*. This is true regardless of where we are in life. Our quality of life is better because we are no longer driven by the emotional residue of those pre-birth experiences. We are more open, emotionally and spiritually, to our own evolution. *We pass on less pain to our children* because our own healing is more complete.

The second, and perhaps even more significant realization, is that we can accompany our children on their journey to birth. We can communicate with them, guide and comfort them through difficult times, and let them know that they are already loved. We can tell them that they are needed and welcome in this world.

Retroactively for ourselves, and *proactively* for our children, we can be born whole.

A Sweatlodge Vision

The story below was pivotal in my growth as I gained a deeper appreciation of the skills I was beginning to take for granted.

It's good to be in a sweatlodge again, to let go of the external world and be in the power of the darkness, the heat, the drumming, the songs, and the prayers. I have attended these ceremonies for several years. I have always found them to be beautiful and powerful times of healing, sharing, and guidance.

The sweatlodge is about ten feet in diameter. Its skeleton is a frame of sticks that have been ceremonially bent, stuck in the ground, and tied together in the shape of an inverted bowl. The cover and door are made of layers of blankets, enough of them that no light penetrates. We crawl through the small doorway when we enter, moving sunwise around the inside of the lodge (this direction is also known as "clockwise"; did you know that the hands of a clock move that way because that's the direction that shadows move on a sunny day?).

In the center of the lodge is a shallow pit. Not far outside the entrance, there is a fire with rocks that have been heating for close to two hours. We enter and sit in a circle inside the lodge. I have been given the honor of keeping the fire. This includes the responsibility of carrying the rocks (the "Old Ones") from the fire to the sweatlodge entrance. Pat, the elder who is conducting the ceremony, uses two forked sticks to maneuver them into the central pit. He places the first five deliberately, one in the center and four more in the directions of east, south, west, and north. For this first round, I bring three more stones after the first five—eight rocks in all. The people in the lodge greet the rocks as I bring them in, much as one would welcome revered elders.

After bringing the rocks to the door, I put more wood on the fire to keep the other Old Ones smiling (red hot). Then I enter the lodge, and when Pat gives the word, I bring the door down to begin the first of the four rounds.

The inside of the lodge is lightless except for the dim glow of the red-hot rocks. My mind knows that this small dome is close to capacity with ten of us in it, yet I feel vast space around me, filled with energies and spirits.

There is a sputtering hiss as Pat pours water onto the rocks. Steam comes down over our heads like a hot, heavy blanket. We lose track of whether the water running on our bodies is condensation or perspiration. The darkness and heat,

Pat's words, drumbeats, and songs move us into an altered state of consciousness.

In the second round of the ceremony, I see in the blackness the spirit of an osprey come down to land gently beside a young woman, resting with her and leaning in with a message. Two other spirits come in as well, to be with two young men in the lodge. I have never met any of these young people before today, yet I am told why each of them is being visited by a particular animal spirit. I am also instructed to ask permission to share the information.

When the door flap is thrown back to signal the end of the second round, I tell Pat that I have something to offer the three young people and ask his permission to share. After a brief moment, in which I sense him checking with his own guides, Pat says, "Please." I speak about what I saw and its meaning. The messages are of affirmation and encouragement for these young people. Later, I find out that they are all in difficult circumstances—"youth at risk" is the current term—and I understand better the messages and their importance.

After the ceremony, we emerge into a bright and beautiful summer day, shifting from one world to another. We're hot and sweaty. Some of us use a handy garden hose for a welcome cold rinse. As we dry ourselves, one of the women who was in the ceremony says to me, "That's a great gift you have."

For a moment I am in a state of confusion. Then I realize that she is referring to my sharing of what I saw in the second round, and I respond, "Thank you." That is all there is to say because for me this is not a great gift. It is a learned and practiced skill, and it is accessible to all of us.

I believe that everyone has the ability to experience the realms beyond the physical. Consider this analogy. We are born with the ability to run. I remember hearing that children rarely walk instead of run before the age of four. Once they're able to move on two feet, they run.

We all started with this ability. Some of us are naturally able to run faster than others. Others, regardless of whether they can outrun their peers, decide there is something about running that draws them. They become joggers or competitive runners. And there are those who want to improve their ability to run.

They find themselves a coach. With the help of their coach, they develop higher speed and greater endurance.

From among the dedicated runners come the elite, the champions.

Just as we all have the ability to run, we all have the ability to connect with a spiritual life. Some find that the spiritual aspect contains something meaningful for them. They take up a spiritual path or develop the spiritual aspect of their lives through religion, meditation, shamanic training, time in nature, or other practice.

Some choose to find a teacher. They learn concepts and techniques for strengthening their spiritual consciousness and power. They train for spiritual development in the same way that a runner trains to improve speed and endurance.

Out of that group of spiritual practitioners emerge those who become the analogy of elite runners: spiritual leaders, shamans, or holy people.

The key point is that spiritual development is available to all of us. I have had students whose ability is an astonishing delight to observe. I have also had students who struggle every step of the way, and whose courage and determination have inspired me.

The Arc of My Journey

No doubt you have heard or read stories about people born with the gift of clear and strong spiritual awareness. That was not me. When I was thirteen, I had my first powerful spiritual experience in nature. I was alone in a canoe, fishing on a lake I knew well in the northwest corner of Ontario in Canada. There were no human roads, habitations, or structures for several miles around, except for a few cabins on the north shore of the lake about a mile away.

I had been at that lake for two months every summer since the age of six. My relationship with the natural world began there. On the water by myself in a rowboat or canoe, I was at home.

From time to time I would experience a connection with nature that transcended the physical senses. In those moments I felt at one with nature's way of being and with the cycles of days, seasons, creation, growth, and death. Eventually, that feeling came to me whenever I sought solitude on the water. I associated being alone in nature with safety, acceptance, serenity, adventure, and beauty.

This day was warm and calm. I was at peace, focused on the meditatively repetitive motions and anticipation of fishing. Suddenly I felt a powerful presence that seemed to be *in* the rocks of the shore. I had no teachings or beliefs that would help me to understand this vivid perception. In my mind I tried to find some physical sign—a noise or a motion—that would indicate a bear or another large animal just out of sight in the bush.

Nothing appeared. The feeling got stronger, and I became frightened. I forgot about fishing and paddled away. I avoided that spot for years.

After the experience near the rock bank, my spiritual life was nearly empty for thirty years. I forgot the experience and devoted my time to education, marriage, career, and family. To feed my imagination, I read books about science fiction, the paranormal, and speculations about our origins.

In early adulthood I lived in the physical realm. Much of my energy outside of work was devoted to dealing with a severely handicapped son, in a time and place where services were minimal. Within that context, I was on the path of material success. I no longer had a strong connection with nature. I had no spiritual path at all. At that time I could not recognize that something was missing in my life, much less articulate it.

However, I continued to have contact with nature, which saved me from losing touch with something I still knew was important. I would take long walks or runs, leaving the trails to explore and find more of the solitude that had been my refuge as a boy. I made occasional canoe trips, alone and with others. I studied books to learn about edible and medicinal plants and mushrooms. My only connection with the spiritual was the time that I spent alone.

Then, after a winter camping trek, my brother showed me a book by Tom Brown Jr. I was riveted from the first page. I had never found any other writing that weaved together the spiritual and physical aspects of life so seamlessly. I knew that I had to learn from this man.

At Tom Brown's Tracker School,[2] I began studying ancient survival techniques. I discovered how to build a shelter that would keep me comfortable in any weather with no fire, how to find and purify water, how to create fire without matches, how to identify and read animal tracks, and how to identify and use many more edible and medicinal wild plants than I already knew.

These teachings come from many peoples who live close to the Earth, primarily those of the Native peoples of North America, known to many of them as Turtle Island. Tom Brown was taught by an Apache elder named Stalking Wolf, who had left his people to wander and learn. Stalking Wolf [3] desired to find the essential truth in any teachings he could find. Nearly sixty years later, he met Tom Brown. They spent ten years together. This is the lineage of my first teachings of these ancient skills and philosophy.

At the end of the week-long course at the Tracker School I experienced my first sweatlodge. After the ceremony I received a vision that has guided my life since then. The story of that experience is in *appendix 1*.

In the years that followed I attended advanced classes at the Tracker School, acquiring higher levels of skill in both the physical and spiritual realms. I learned to enter a state of deep meditation in which I was aware of energies and beings outside the realm of ordinary physical existence. I learned to journey spiritually in nonphysical realms through purposeful dynamic meditation, to communicate with spiritual entities, and to use nonphysical energy for healing. I came to have a deep appreciation of the power of ceremony.

There are two important differences between dynamic meditation and the passive meditative practices that are more contemplative in their approach.

The first is that dynamic meditation has a purpose or an intention, which is held in awareness before the journey begins. It is often verbalized and is then released.

The second difference is that dynamic meditation involves a deliberate journey and a destination. I would begin the journey by visualizing moving on a pathway or stairs, flying, or progressing in some other fashion. When I had arrived at the destination, I would re-engage with the purpose of the journey.

I learned to communicate with the spirits of nonhuman beings and developed a deep spiritual connection with my nonhuman relatives in the natural world. I have had an affinity and spiritual relationship with plants, trees, and objects such as stones for many years. They have taught me about patience, acceptance, purpose, generosity, forgiveness, perspective, and most of all the unified consciousness that we all share.

I learned to travel in spirit to places that are inaccessible to me in my physical form.

The abilities to travel and to communicate spiritually with beings whose consciousness is very unlike that of humans were essential in the research described in this book.

It was in a meditation that I met the brightest, most beautiful, and most powerful spirit I have ever encountered. It identified itself to me as Jesus Christ. That memory still moves me deeply. In that experience I came to know in a powerful way that I *matter*, that I have a place and a role in this universe. I know that I am cared *about* and cared *for* by loving powers beyond my ability to comprehend.

After some years on this path, I believed that I was the only one in my part of the world who had the physical and spiritual skills I was developing. Thus, I decided to begin teaching so I could be with people who shared my passion, people with whom I could talk and practice with. I also knew that this was the best way to avoid losing my own skills. I could only build so many shelters and fires without someone there to share the work and the accomplishment!

I began with small workshops on various topics that included making fire, identifying and using edible and medicinal plants, building shelters, and tracking animals. Soon I expanded those training sessions into weekend workshops.

When I was ready, I began teaching a spiritual path based on what I had learned from Tom Brown and amplified by other teachings and my own experience.

A year after my first class at Tracker School, I met a teacher, an Anicinabe man acknowledged by his people to be a medicine man. I attended sweat-lodge ceremonies with him, and he guided my first Vision Quest.

The Vision Quest is a ceremony that has been known for thousands of years by cultures around the world. Participants prepare ceremonially, sometimes for several months or years (one man said to me, "I spent four days on the hill. It took me twenty years to get there"). They are guided by elders who have walked that same road for themselves. A common format is to spend four days of solitude in nature asking, praying, and listening for guidance or a vision. During that time they are without food, without human company, without distractions, and with only minimal shelter.

Like many transformational experiences, the Vision Quest must be lived to be understood. In *appendix 2,* I offer a description of my most powerful Vision Quest. I received two gifts there. One was a new sweatlodge ceremony. The other was the ability to draw the essence of water into my body when I could not drink.

In the seven years that I walked with him, my Anicinabe teacher also prepared me to conduct sweatlodge ceremonies and to guide Vision Quests.

During those years I learned the ways of respect and the talking circle, the ceremonies of daily life, and the ceremonies and responsibilities of the sweatlodge. I made a commitment to honor these ways by keeping them for the generations yet to be born.

Along the way I also gained attunement at the second level of Reiki.

I once asked my Anicinabe teacher, "How do you respond when people ask you if you're a medicine man?"

He said, "I tell them, 'There are those who say that I am.'" In his tradition, and in the tradition carried by Tom Brown Jr., it is not considered appropriate for someone to proclaim themselves as a shaman or a medicine person. In those traditions, recognition of that status can only come from the community.

Not all traditions share this practice. There are cultures, in Latin America and South America as well as in other parts of the world, where people who have been initiated have no hesitation about claiming their status and responsibilities as shamans.

I love the role of teacher. I am a teacher of spirituality and awakening, a teacher of life advancement through coaching, and a teacher of wellness through my work as a healer.

Guinea Pig Number 2

I met Dr. Grant McFetridge in the late 1990s. He had invited me three times to a course on a recently developed healing modality called Emotional Freedom Techniques or EFT, also known as Tapping. EFT is discussed in detail in chapter 6. I declined his first two invitations, but after the third (three is my command number for paying attention), I attended his one-day course.

I did not understand how this strange-looking technique could work, but at the same time, I was impressed by how effective it was, and intrigued since the Native North American shamanic path I had followed for ten years did not incorporate the concept of energy meridians and their potential in healing.

During the next few years I studied and practiced EFT intensively. This proved to be an important tool in the work Grant and I were to do together.

After the EFT course, Grant said he thought I might be interested in a project he had recently designed.

He said he had talked with many people who had had peak experiences. The experience might be a flash of profound awareness or wisdom, a momentary sense of deep connection with other-than-human beings, an awareness of flows of energy moving through and around us, or an ability to see beauty in all people and all things.

For almost everyone, these experiences lasted only a short time. The person might wish or try to get them back, but they often felt out of reach.

I understood what he was saying. Most of my peak experiences had come during meditations, in the sweatlodge, or on Vision Quests. Some had lasted for several days; however, all but one had ended, and even that one was not continuous.

Grant described his idea that *ongoing* peak states of awareness are available to all of us, but are blocked by traumas that occur before we are even born. He invited me to join him in investigating his theory and finding ways to heal the injuries that can occur before birth. If his theory was correct, healing those injuries for myself might allow me to experience an ongoing peak state.

I felt that much of what I had learned in the past twenty years was good preparation for my role in the project.

Grant asked me to help him explore the part of our life's journey that begins with the creation of sperm cell and egg cell and ends with birth. I would enter a deep meditation, and he would guide me to the developmental events that he was interested in: conception, implantation in the wall of the womb, and the first contraction of labor. I would describe what I saw and felt. I was fascinated, and so agreed to be his test subject. I was interested in exploring life in the womb firsthand, and in the potential benefits of applying EFT to healing the trauma and injury that may occur before birth. I was also intrigued by the possibility of experiencing stable peak states for myself. I was ready for my job as experimental subject, object, *and* witness. I was ready to be Guinea Pig #2.

(Guinea Pig #1 was a woman who worked briefly with Grant in the earliest stages of the project. She was unable to devote more than a little time at the beginning of the research.)

Navigating a Different World

Initially, the biggest challenge for me was believing that what Grant wanted to do was even possible. This was new territory for both of us. In retrospect, none of it was out of reach. Once we had blazed the trails, they were easy to find again and follow. I believe now that these techniques can be learned by anyone.

In order to access the locations in space and time that he had in mind, I would need four distinct skills. The first skill was to move my consciousness to a different location. That part would be easy. I had learned to "travel in spirit" to gather information from locations that I had not visited in my physical body. One of the exciting aspects of this was that in this work, the "different location" was my mother's womb!

I would also be required to travel backward in time more than fifty years to my own conception and gestation. This too would be easy. I was familiar with temporal regression through my practice of EFT as well as through my shamanic work.

The third skill was communicating with organisms whose consciousness would be very different from mine. I was confident that I could communicate with the sperm cell, egg cell, and growing fetus since I had previously learned to communicate with other non-human beings.

The fourth requirement initially looked much more difficult. Grant's intention was that I would take on the first-person perspective of the egg, sperm, or embryo. In other words, I would attempt to perceive *through the consciousness of that organism.* I would try to see what it saw, feel what it felt, respond as it responded. I would not attempt to control it, but experience what *it* did in a fashion that was so intimate that it would be *my* experience as well.

As you will read in the section below titled *Differences in Perception from Ordinary Consciousness*, I succeeded beyond what I had initially hoped.

This may have been easier than expected because it was my own self that I was experiencing rather than the identity of another being or person.

Trailblazing

During the next several years, Grant and I got together from time to time at various locations in Canada and the United States so he could verbally guide me to specific points in the pre-birth experience as I entered a deep meditative state. He would direct me to describe what I saw and felt while he recorded, made notes, and occasionally took photos. We would often work for ten hours a day, and I might be in an altered state for as much as five days. The work was exciting because we were in territory that as far as we knew had never been explored before. It was also rewarding because it felt like we were making significant discoveries nearly every day. We felt like trailblazers.

Once in a while someone has the privilege of being a true trailblazer. I did not know at the time whether this was so for me; it may have been more that I was like the first one to go through a landscape after a snowfall, where you realize only after the snow melts that a trail has been made by many earlier feet. But if you believe that you are the first person ever to be there, the feeling of excitement and the feeling of discovery are the same as if you truly were the first. In the moment of the experience, you cannot know. You must wait until the snow melts, until you find the stories of those who have been there before you.

As I began to write this book, I discovered accounts by people who had indeed explored parts of this same territory. Some of them have written about their journeys. Others have described models that assist our understanding of the pre-birth experience.[4]

It was affirming to discover that their experiences were like mine. And it was exhilarating to realize that Grant and I truly did create and blaze trails into previously unexplored territory.

At the beginning our relationship was that of researcher and subject. Over time, we became collaborating colleagues, then friends.

We generally followed the timeline of development in the research. We started with my pre-conception identities: sperm cell and egg cell. In separate journeys, I re-experienced my own conception (it still feels odd to say that!) as though I were the sperm cell, then the egg cell. Then, I experienced again my implantation as a zygote in the wall of my mother's womb. During the next two years of the research, I revisited these early experiences a number of times and explored the months of my gestation and the time of labor.

Not all of the experiences were beautiful or even pleasant. Some were extremely painful, emotionally and psychically, and I eventually had to withdraw from the research because of that.

In telling this story I will follow the linear chronology of development of a baby—me—*in utero.*

There was also one fascinating side trip later in the project. I began this particular journey as before, starting as the egg in my mother's ovary. This time, however, I moved *backward* in time to explore the creation of my own self as the egg. I describe that journey in *appendix 3*.

An Introduction to Brainwaves[5]

This is a brief overview of the five bands of electromagnetic waves generated by human brains. I offer this material so you will recognize the terms when they appear later in the book.

In general, the slower brain waves are associated with deeper meditative states.

Gamma – 38 Hz (cycles per second) and higher

Gamma waves, the fastest brainwaves, have only recently been discovered because of their very low amplitude, so they are not yet thoroughly understood. These waves appear to be associated with heightened perception and expanded consciousness, or a peak mental state, when the brain is simultaneously processing information in different areas.

Beta – 12 to 38 Hz

Beta waves dominate normal waking consciousness. They are produced during active thinking activities, such as solving problems, making judgments and decisions, focusing on tasks, and engaging actively with surroundings.

Alpha – 8 to 12 Hz

Alpha waves are associated with a calm, relaxed state of mind: the resting state of the brain. These waves occur during light meditative and mindful activities, or quietly flowing thoughts. This state is also associated with artistic creativity and being "in the zone. Alpha waves indicate mental calmness with alertness, mind/body integration and learning.

Theta – 3 to 8 Hz

Theta waves occur in dreaming sleep and in deep meditation. They can also be produced during free-flowing, unconscious thought that can occur while doing automatic tasks. In Theta, the senses are less aware of the external world and more focused within. This is also the twilight state, experienced during coming awake or drifting off to sleep.

In Theta it is common to experience vivid imagery and intuition, and to receive information and insights from beyond our normal conscious awareness.

Delta – 0.5 to 3 Hz

Delta waves are low brain waves generated during dreamless sleep and in the deepest meditative states. This is the state of awareness of the nonphysical or spiritual realms. In the Delta state, we are generally not aware of our physical body or environment.

When I guide journeys into the realm between lives, I begin by taking clients into the Delta state through a process that requires forty-five minutes to an hour. Attaining this state is necessary in order to enter the realm of souls. The process is similar to what I followed on my journeys to be with my pre-birth self.

The client leaves behind most of their connection with the physical world and in particular the need of the mind to understand and control their circumstances. With good guidance, almost all of us are capable of making this transition.

As mentioned above, after practicing meditation for several years, I was able to enter states of deep meditation quickly and consistently. Initially, I used visualization and a drumbeat. Eventually, I could make the transition without those props, using only a simple breathing technique.

I learned to function physically in the Theta state, though the air felt as thick as syrup and I had to move slowly in order not to make a mistake, even when doing something as simple as preparing a cup of tea. When I spoke in this state, I had the feeling that I was not quite of this world, that someone else's mouth was expressing thoughts that I knew originated in my mind.

In the even deeper Delta state, my awareness was disengaged from the physical world to the extent that I was mostly unaware of my surroundings and almost completely unable to move. It was in this state that I did most of my work with Grant.

Although my awareness and perceptions were almost entirely of the nonphysical realm, I found that I could speak, with considerable effort in the beginning and then more easily with practice, allowing me to describe to Grant what I was observing and feeling. It was as though my consciousness occupied two compartments. In one compartment, the part of my consciousness that was in Delta experienced a reality that was completely detached from the physical. From the other compartment, as though through a doorway, the part of my consciousness that was in the Alpha state was observing and describing the Delta experience to Grant.

Later, I learned that distinct parts of the brain can simultaneously produce different frequencies of brain waves. This allowed one part of my awareness to be in Delta and another part in Alpha. It provides an explanation for what I was able to do.

Differences in Perception from Ordinary Consciousness

Four features of my experience in the womb differed from what is present in ordinary consciousness: size, identity, time, and space.

Anyone learning to do this work must adjust to these differences. Fortunately, the adjustment is easy to make after the initial strangeness.

Size

On my meditative journeys, everything around me appeared normal in magnitude from the point of view I held in the moment. When I took on the identity of the egg and saw from that perspective, the approaching sperm cells looked like tiny hyperactive tadpoles. When I "became" the sperm, the egg appeared immense and the other sperm cells were the same size as I.

These different perspectives were disorienting at first. They reminded me of astronomical displays illustrating the relative sizes of Earth (tiny) beside Jupiter (huge), then Jupiter (tiny) beside the sun (huge), then the sun beside a blue giant star, that star within a galaxy, and so on.

From previous experiences I knew that this was a natural aspect of meditative journeys to environments that are physically very small or very large in comparison with our physical bodies. That helped me to adjust to the differences in scale as I moved my point of view back and forth from sperm to egg.

After conception, there was only the one viewpoint of the growing embryo, rather than the two of egg and sperm. That was both less exciting and less confusing.

Identity

I could choose between two points of view: the organism in the womb (egg, sperm, zygote, or fetus) and that of my adult self.

When I took the viewpoint of the organism, everything was a new, completely absorbing first-person experience of *now*. Then when I shifted from there to being my adult self, I felt like an outside observer. From that point of view, I had the advantage of several decades of life experience. I was more aware of a larger context and less absorbed in the moment.

It was as though I were watching a play in which I was also the main actor where I could perceive from either the place of the actor or a member of the audience. Either point of view was possible and I could change from one to the other instantaneously.

As the observing adult, I also had absolute confidence that I would survive. If I had not survived, I would not be there to observe my pre-birth self!

After I had been doing this work for several months, I found that the distinction between my fetal self and my adult self disappeared. There was no longer a sense of separation; it was all simply and wonderfully *me*. It remains so today.

Time and Space

In the meditations I was not limited by three-dimensional space or time. I could move from any moment and any location in space to any other with no sense of discontinuity.

For some readers this may give rise to a question: how is it possible to have a sense of moving back and forth in time when it is said of higher planes of consciousness that there is no time or space there?

It is true that there is a state of consciousness in which the concepts of space and time are genuinely without meaning. This state is often called Awareness, Unity, or Oneness.

In these meditative journeys I did not move into that level. I was in a realm that in a sense is one level down from the place of Unity. In the realm I was in, time does exist in the sense that I perceived events as occurring in sequence. Even so, any moment that I chose to visit was the *present* moment to my perception. The experience was not like a memory; rather, it was a genuine *re*-experiencing in what I perceived as real time.

In this state, I was able to move to different moments in time through nothing more than an exercise of intent. If I wanted to be at a chosen point in time in the womb or at a specific developmental event, I was there with no effort and no feeling of having made a transition.

Space also exists in this realm in that I perceived a "here" and a "there." In other words, I had a sense of location. As with time, it was possible to move between locations in space without effort and without limitation.

These two critical differences made it possible to shift in time from being myself as an adult to being an egg cell (*the* egg cell), and to shift in space from the couch my body was on to the womb of my mother with no sense of displacement or incongruity.

It was not that time or space ceased to have reality or meaning, but that my journeys were not subject to the limitations of ordinary three-dimensional physical existence. This was possible because I was experiencing a different kind of reality.

PART 2

THREE UNIVERSAL DEVELOPMENTAL EVENTS

Chapter 1: The Journey to Conception

Chapter 1 is about how we get started: the journeys of egg and sperm cells from their creation to the moment of conception, including some of the difficult or traumatic aspects of those journeys and how those issues were healed. I also describe what this journey was like for me.

The Beginning of the Journey of the Egg

Both sperm and egg, even before conception, are on the journey of life. Their purpose from the time they come into being is clear. It is to grow, learn, meet challenges, and become someone wonderful.

Imagine your maternal grandmother pregnant with your mother. As the fetus that would become your mother developed through the nine months before she was born, special cells were formed in *her* tiny womb. Years later, when your mother reached puberty, these cells would become viable egg cells. One of them was the egg that joined with a sperm cell from your father to become *you*.

Twenty-seven years before I was conceived, the egg that became me was formed within the womb of my grandmother, in the fetus that would become my mother!

When Grant and I began our research project, we did not begin at that earliest time. We instead chose a time about midway through my mother's menstrual cycle when her body began to prepare for ovulation by choosing which egg to release—the Chosen One among the eggs, destined to unite with the Chosen One among the sperm.

I began the journey by using visualizations and breathing techniques to enter a deep meditative state. Guided by Grant, I moved to the selected point in time and found myself in my mother's left ovary just as her ovulation began. I perceived all around me as though I were the size of an egg cell. Then with a thrill I understood that I *was* an egg cell, and that I was the Chosen One.

The moment when a particular egg is chosen to be released into the Fallopian tube is charged with anticipation and excitement. I was aware that I would not die and be released from the body as the lining of the womb was sloughed off in menstruation. Instead, I would be *fulfilled*. I would unite with a sperm cell, and in so doing, I would attain my purpose.

There was a beautiful innocence in this time. There was also a sense that I was loved by something immense, sacred, and powerful—a Mother of cosmic magnitude who cared about more than words can express. The feeling was like that of the *Hallelujah Chorus* from Handel's *Messiah*, amplified many times. It was a moment of indescribable rejoicing.

Eventually I came to understand that this anticipation and excitement happens every time the womb prepares to release an egg, whether or not the egg experiences conception. I also came to understand that the Mother is Gaia (more on this later).

From a spiritual point of view, I the egg was held energetically within an enclosing sphere of white energy. Yet there was no sense of being protected, and therefore no sense that there was anything to be protected *from*.

I was in a continuous state of bliss! Up to the time of release from my mother's left ovary, I was unaware of anything outside myself except love, other eggs, and a shared sense of destiny. I felt an absolute conviction that something momentous would happen soon. I was in a state of Oneness with all of creation—a beautiful experience of community consciousness.

It is no wonder that I, like many of us, yearn in our adult lives for that state of Oneness. We have known it already.

When I revisited this occasion later, I realized that these were some of the best, and last, moments of pure wonder for the egg. This wonder was almost completely unaffected by my mother's life experience or her emotions.

I understood that the unripe eggs within a female baby are not sufficiently developed to be affected by the stresses of that baby's birth. They do not remember their mother's birth because they are in a state of deep dormancy that will not end until the girl's body reaches puberty.

Into the Fallopian Tube

The development of the ego, which is so necessary for life, begins before conception for both egg and sperm. For me, as for all eggs, this process of psychological and emotional growth and strengthening began at the time of release from my place in the ovary.

Up to this moment, I had developed in an environment of safety and comfort.[6] Now that I was ready to deal with the challenges of conception, I left behind the familiar environment where I had spent my first years of existence (remember, my mother was twenty-seven when I was conceived). This minuscule being that was me—about one tenth of a millimeter or the thickness of a human hair in diameter, yet still by far the biggest cell in my mother's body—was brushed into the Fallopian tube. There I awaited the arrival of the sperm cell that would merge with me.

I encountered a whole new range of experiences. One was separation from the serene and beautiful environment of the ovary. Another was exposure to—immersion in!—new hormones and chemicals, which I perceived as odors. They pervaded my entire being with new and sometimes unpleasant effects.

Sensing unfamiliar movement, I felt uncertain, which was unlike any sensation I had known before. Yet the impression was not frightening. It was like the first day of a new beginning. Remember your first day at school or university or your first time in a sports tournament? Most likely you were looking forward to the event, but could not imagine it because you'd never been there before. It was like that for me as I entered the Fallopian tube.

Then Grant instructed me to move ahead in time, to a few moments before conception.

I suddenly found myself in a state of excited anticipation! I *knew* that something magnificent was about to happen.[7] I *knew* that I would unite with another, and that he[8] was on his way to me.

As an adult I had read that there are millions of sperm cells "competing" to fertilize the egg. Yet as the egg in that moment, conscious of the sperm cells all around me, I did not have a feeling that they were competing with each other. I knew which one I would join with. The choice had already been made by a power greater than either the sperm or I, greater than even my mother. My role was to surrender actively, to carry out my part in the unfolding of this wonderful event.

As The One Sperm approached, I felt purpose and anticipation. At the moment of conception, as

I enfolded the head of the sperm cell into my body, I felt absolute fulfillment—and profound violation.

The Journey of the Sperm Cell

The coming into existence of the sperm cell that became me was in many respects like the coming into existence of the egg that became me. The sperm's journey began in the body of my paternal grandmother when she became pregnant with the male baby who would be my father. As this male fetus developed in her womb, cells were formed in the tiny testicles of that tiny fetus. After my father reached puberty, these "germ cells" divided and produced viable sperms. One of them was the sperm that joined with the egg cell from my mother to create me.

Sperm cells come into full maturity over a time of about ten weeks—up to a hundred million per day. Within the body of the father, the cells are viable for about five days. If the sperm is introduced into a woman's body during this period, the nutrients there can keep it alive for up to five more days.

My journey as the sperm cell was similar to my journey as the egg in other respects as well—leaving a safe and familiar place, adjusting to a new environment, and facing an unpredictable new experience. For me as the sperm, however, the uncertainty was mostly dispelled by urgency. I was driven by an irresistible impulse to *move* and a powerful intention to be The One.

After I had entered a deep meditative state for this session, Grant directed me to enter the consciousness of the sperm cell that would be The One. For a moment, my rational mind resisted as I could not understand how it was possible for me to know which sperm that would be. Then I effortlessly found myself in the consciousness of one sperm cell.

Immediately, I knew I was not just any sperm cell. I was The One. Among all those others, I was destined to become a fully formed human.

I was excited to know that I was The One. I did not know, nor did I care, whether every other sperm cell might also feel that same way. I was not interested in them. I regarded them as my competitors in this final stage of my journey to conception, and I felt the triumph of my imminent victory.

Later, when I revisited the journey of sperm cells, I discovered that we were working in concert. This was contrary to what I had assumed to be true. I had thought that we were all in do-or-die competition against each other. For many of us this was true, as we swam vigorously toward the egg. But when I went back again to that moment, I realized that some sperm cells give up their own sense of purpose to assist others. The discovery that they gave their lives to help me toward my destiny was humbling for my adult consciousness.

For me, and for all other sperm cells there was no question about the direction in which we needed to move. I felt my own strength and purpose, and felt that same strength and purpose in other sperms around me.

As he had done with the egg, Grant then instructed me to move to a moment just before conception.

I became aware of the egg as a glowing and inviting presence ahead. She felt like a loving mother calling me home. I was welcomed, taken in, enfolded, and fulfilled—and I was annihilated.

Conception: Violation and Annihilation, or a Royal Wedding?

For both sperm and egg, joining together at conception is simultaneously traumatic and wondrous.

The trauma is an almost complete loss of individuality with a feeling of destruction on one side and violation on the other. The intensity of this experience, particularly at this early stage of existence, is greater than anything we have experienced before.

Grant's intent in this meditation was to investigate the traumatic aspects of the coming together of egg and sperm. From his point of view the experiment was a success. For me, having been deliberately guided to experience the traumatic aspects of conception, the unexpected pain was extreme.

I wanted to be free of that pain. After conception, I wanted my fetal self to not be affected by that earliest trauma, and I wanted the healing for the benefit of my adult self as well. So, soon after this journey through the experience of conception, I revisited the event on my own with Grant nearby. I healed the sense of violation on one side and annihilation on the other, applying the process described in chapter 5.

When I did so, my perception changed profoundly. The sensations of trauma were gone. I understood that it was necessary for the sperm and egg cell to lose their identities in order that a new being could be created.

After this healing, the event of conception had the feeling of a royal wedding where I was both bride and groom. It was the most beautiful of experiences, like an exquisitely choreographed slow-motion dance.

I felt the loving support, pride, and pleasure of many beings joined in a great chorus of celebration. Then I became aware of another, even grander presence. This was the unified consciousness of the Earth, a single being that I instantly knew as Gaia.

The Gaia hypothesis, developed and refined by James Lovelock and Lynn Margulis fifty years ago, is named for the Greek goddess who personified the Earth. Its central idea is that the organic and inorganic components of planet Earth have evolved together as a single living, self-regulating system. This living system automatically regulates global temperature, atmospheric content, ocean salinity, and many other factors in order to maintain its own habitability. "Life maintains conditions suitable for its own survival."

The living system of Earth can be thought of as analogous to any organism, which is capable of controlling its own body temperature, blood salinity, and so on in order to maintain health. As an example of adaptation by the Earth to changing conditions, consider this: the luminosity of the sun has increased by about 30 percent since life began almost four billion years ago, yet the system (i.e., Gaia) has responded in such a way as to keep surface temperatures at levels that support organic life.[9]

My experience of Gaia includes all this and more. When I met her (definitely female!), the immense Gaia consciousness transcended and included the individual consciousnesses of all other beings, organic and inorganic. She felt like an adoring grandmother, ancient and eternally youthful, surrounded by her family.

Below are the words that I spoke as I completed the healing of the traumas of my conception.[10]

The music is part of me now.

Conception is a moment of triumph. It is an enormous expansion.

Conception is one of the highlights of our entire existence. There are two entities, both of whom are whole, and they are merging. WOW! It's like this intense huge golden light.

I'm swamped—immersed in it like it has no end.

I felt rapturous. There was a shared feeling of joy and accomplishment among all observing consciousnesses. Many of the witnesses were sperm cells. They joined in the celebration of the union, the crossing of the threshold of creation. None of them felt disappointment or sadness when it became evident that they were not to be the "groom"—only delight for The One and for the success of conception. This was pure attainment of destiny.

It is not surprising that sometimes the mother herself is aware of the moment of conception!

And almost immediately, of course, there were other impulses, other guidance and imperatives to be followed.

Chapter 2: Implantation in the Uterine Wall

This chapter is a discussion of my experience with another significant developmental event: implantation as an embryo in the wall of my mother's uterus.

The first few phases of cell division from fertilized egg to blastocyst, and the event of implantation in the wall of my mother's uterus, were unremarkable by comparison with conception. Unremarkable, but not without their own elements of stress.

After I the egg had joined with me the sperm, I as the newly formed zygote was uncertain whether I would successfully implant in my mother's womb. Driven by the impulse to become anchored, I felt that I knew *what* needed to be done but not *how*. As it happened, I didn't need to figure anything out. I approached the wall of the uterus and the attachment was done, making this developmental event effortless.

I was swimming in an ocean surf as an adult a while ago and was surprised by a large double wave. I found that I could enjoy being tumbled by the power of the ocean because I knew that there was solid ground under me, and I was confident I would soon be able to stand up.

Implantation was like that. In a similar fashion to being tumbled in the surf, though without quite the same degree of confidence (it was, after all, the first time for implantation!), I the embryo found the experience exhilarating. This feeling was echoed in the experience with the ocean wave.

The months from implantation to birth were an exciting time of progress and learning as I developed the physical senses and awareness that we take so much for granted as adults. Every day, though I did not feel the passage of time, I became *more*. These new sensations, and my increasing abilities to perceive and integrate them, felt normal and even beautiful.

I now understand that it was in the fifth month of gestation that my soul (see chapter 4) integrated with my body. My soul and my human self worked together to develop a strong and mutually beneficial relationship between the two. At the time, what I experienced was a powerful feeling of *rightness* about what was occurring.

I also understood that Gaia, my mother, and I were all cocreators of who I was becoming. I knew that even in difficult circumstances, the love a mother has for the baby in her womb helps both of them to live and grow.

In my work with Grant, we did not spend much time studying specific stages of gestation after implantation. The stresses I experienced during this time were more related to my mother's ongoing emotional, mental, and physical experience. This aspect of my journey is discussed in chapter 5

Chapter 3: The First Contraction of Labor

This chapter tells about my experience with the most difficult moment of life for a fetus: the first hard contraction. I tell the story of my experience of that time and how Gaia assisted me through it..

This chapter also tells how I applied retroactive healing techniques to heal the trauma of the first contraction.

As I approached the time of my birth, I felt once again that something momentous was about to happen. Bathed in a new assortment of hormones, accompanied by new emotions in my mother, I felt gentle contractions as her uterus prepared for delivery. I sensed that a new phase of my journey was imminent. These first mild contractions felt different from what I was accustomed to in the normal course of the day, though they were initially only slightly more vigorous.

I was not prepared for the first hard contraction. I as the baby was initially terrified. I felt crushed and suffocated, even though I was still immersed in amniotic fluid and not yet breathing, by a uterine wall that had suddenly become hard. I was unable to move.

Even in my distress, I knew this was how it was supposed to happen and felt that something bigger was comforting me and helping me through my fear. Again, the source of this comfort was the collective consciousness of all living beings on this planet—Gaia. My own soul was also present (the concept of souls is discussed in chapter 4).

The following is an edited transcript of the words I spoke as I experienced the first hard contraction.

"Gaia, you promised me that you would be with me!"

Now I hear again from Gaia something that I misunderstood the first time. It is "You have to do this by yourself," and not "You have to do this alone."

Gaia says to me, "Little one, I'll be with you. You'll see me. You'll know that I'm there."

I can't believe that. (At this point Grant observed that I appeared quite distraught. I recall those moments as extremely painful. I felt abandoned at a stage when I was confused and helpless.)

There is a message for me . . . it is a message of love that has a fierce quality. It comes from Gaia, who is there with my mother!

Gaia says to me, "It's time to separate from your mother."

I'm calming . . . (sighing)

Gaia lets me be with my mother for a moment. I understand for the first time that my mother and I are two distinct physical beings.

There is also something about us that is indivisible . . . we are doing this together.

I see one of those waves coming (this is a description of how I perceived the messages from Gaia. They looked like ocean swells). I know what it means. The physical message is "Move. Begin to move."

From this point on, I was in the process of being born. It was unpleasant. I felt rejected, expelled from a place where I had been safe. I felt betrayed. The world I had known as home was no longer welcoming.

To me as a baby, these were new feelings and I could do nothing to ease them. I could only endure. But to me as the observing adult, the feelings were familiar. I understood at that moment that I had carried the pain of that first rejection and betrayal, as a background feeling of abandonment, through my entire life.

During the birthing process I felt fear. Some of it was my mother's and some of it was mine. Neither of us knew what the outcome would be. For me as the baby, the process was completely unknown territory. My mother's mild apprehension (she had given birth to one other child) fed and magnified my own fear.

By this time I had been working with Grant for several months, and we had developed an effective method for healing *in utero* trauma. Our approach combined meditative regression to the womb with a meridian therapy technique called Emotional Freedom Technique. The method itself, and my experience with it, is discussed in detail in chapter 5 and chapter 6.

As I applied the method, I was aware of the healing of my womb trauma reverberating through my life, up to the present time.

Following my own experience of healing, I refined the method further and began to employ it with clients to heal their pre-birth trauma. I also began to teach it.

As a more mature, more skilled, and more spiritually conscious adult, I was able to be an effective guide to my yet-to-be-born self. This was an essential piece of the healing and of my becoming who I am today. I was reminded of this wisdom from Scott Peck:

The spiritually evolved person is masterful in the same sense that the adult is masterful in relation to the child. Matters that present great problems for the child and cause it great pain may be of no consequence to the adult at all.[11]

PART 3

THE ENVIRONMENT OF THE WOMB

Part 2 discussed three significant developmental events of the time before birth. Part 3 is about a different aspect of that time: the overall physical and emotional environment of the womb.

Chapter 4: Healing *For* and Healing *From* the Pain of Our Mother

In previous chapters I discussed developmental events that occur for all of us before birth and how healing may be needed to relieve the traumatic burden of those events. Once healed, I discovered how astonishingly beautiful they were.

This chapter is about environmental healing rather than developmental event healing. It presents the story of my experience in the womb from a more general perspective. I discuss the effects of my mother's ongoing stresses, and my healing from those effects.

The Need for Challenge

Why are the hardships of conception, gestation, and labor necessary? Why can't our experience of the time within our mothers be of safety, easy growth, and beauty?

There is a story, whose exact origin I do not remember, from a man who saw a butterfly struggling to emerge from its chrysalis.

He described being touched by what looked to him like a great difficulty, and he decided to make it easier for the butterfly to emerge. However, his help caused the butterfly to die. It had been deprived of the struggle necessary to stretch, inflate, and harden its wings, so it could not fly.

How is this relevant for us humans?

We are born into a world that requires us to be both tough and resilient *when we come in*. The stresses and challenges of the womb, including birth, are necessary in the same way that the struggles of butterfly or dragonfly are necessary: they prepare us for survival.

We need to be able to survive apart from our mothers. As an absolute minimum, we have to be able to breathe and take in nourishment on our own if we are to become independent. We need to be ready to deal with gravity, cold, a new array of sounds, bright light, unfamiliar odors, and other physical discomforts. We need to be able to make the sounds that will communicate our needs.

Our experience in the womb is designed to prepare us for life after birth. From the first unsettling sensation of movement for the egg as it separates from the ovary, and for the sperm the realization that it is one of competing millions, we are exposed to new and higher levels of challenge almost continuously. It is through our responses to these challenges that we build the physical and emotional strength and resilience we will need *just to make it through our birth.*

Through every tiny increment of growth, we transcend our previous selves while including the best of what we have been.

Honor for All Mothers

Even though the challenges of pre-birth life are necessary, we still experience pain and need to heal from it. It is not a mother's fault that her baby experiences pain while in her womb. She is to be honored, not diminished, for providing her baby with the experiences that will prepare it for life.

We live in a time when identifying and punishing the "guilty" pervades societal attitudes and behavior. This is not how we become better people or a better species. We need to offer acceptance rather than blame, and compassion rather than shame, when events unfold less than perfectly. In particular, we need to offer love and support to women who experience the loss of a baby.

To those of you who are or will become mothers, I offer deep respect. Only you truly understand what it is to bear the responsibility of motherhood. You carry and nurture within you for nine months a being which, *if all goes well*, will develop from a single egg, united with a single sperm, into a baby. As one friend said to me, "A mother is a miracle."

I invite you to know that regardless of what you have experienced in your own life, you deserve to respect and love yourself as you do others. In so doing you serve your children and through them all life.

I make the same offer and the same invitation to men who are or may become fathers. As men, it is our responsibility to be as healthy as we can in all dimensions of ourselves. This will enable us to have the good lives we deserve. We will then be able to serve women, children, our communities, and all life in a good way. Perhaps you will resonate with this idea expressed by a Native elder: "Women protect the children. Men protect the village."

My Experience in the Womb

When I regressed to my mother's womb, there was one sensation that was foundational. For almost all my time *in utero* until just before birth, I was in the present, the always-moving, eternal *now*.

During that time I became aware that I am the fusion of a soul and a human being. I knew that my mother, the spirit of Gaia, and I all worked together for my growth as a healthy baby in my mother's womb.

My mother held, protected, and nourished me. My purpose was simple: to grow and to learn. There was no need for me to *do* anything. The flow of growth and learning was effortless. I had no sense of the passage of time, yet every moment was enriched by new physical sensations, expanded awareness, and greater strength. I was, at a deep level within myself, confident. All was as it should be. This belief that all was well on my journey through gestation sustained me through some challenging times.

I have discussed my experience of the trauma of three developmental events earlier in the book. This section is about pain of a different nature.

The relationship between my mother and me was so intimate that her emotional and physical experience was also my experience—almost my *entire* experience. In every moment I felt both my mother's transient feelings and her enduring baseline emotional state. I felt them as though they were my own. When something made her laugh, I was elevated by her joy as well as by the endorphins her system produced. If she was surprised, I felt the same adrenaline that stimulated her. If she was in a state of stress and her system was flooded with cortisol, I felt her stress and my blood was charged with cortisol as well.

I felt the effects of her fluctuating levels of nutrients, toxins, stimulants, even oxygen and carbon dioxide. As she moved, I moved.

I was not stressed the way some fetuses are. My mother did not drink alcohol, smoke, or use drugs. But if she had a strong cup of tea, I was overstimulated. If she was afraid, I was in a state of terror. If she was sad or depressed, I too was in a black pit.

In the womb I also acquired a version of my mother's basic beliefs about the world and herself. This was linked with the emotions that arose from her beliefs. When she saw the world as a good place, I benefitted not only from the serotonin she produced, but also from the energy of her positive thought patterns. When she saw the world as a painful place, I was influenced by that belief as well as by her elevated levels of adrenaline and cortisol.

I was unable to do anything other than be immersed in my mother's experience since I did not have a sufficiently developed mind to assess rightness or wrongness. Without the capacity to detach from what my mother felt or believed, I had no way to know whether what I was experiencing was ordinary or unusual, healthy or destructive. I could not know that my mother's way might not be the only way.

In a rudimentary way, I assumed that the life I experienced in her womb was normal. I also assumed that life was like this not only for me, but for everyone else as well.

Healing the Pain of the Womb

Before I met Grant McFetridge, the possibility that I might need to heal old emotional wounds did not interest me. As a young person I had abundant energy and believed that there were more enjoyable, constructive things to do than explore and heal long-ago wounds that I didn't believe in anyway.

Then, as I neared fifty, life presented me with a series of events in which I both caused and received deep emotional pain. Those incidents forced me to make a choice either to continue to run from my pain or to turn and face it.

Deciding that I wanted to be free of the pain, I accepted the truth that "the only way out is through." I devoured books and articles, seeking to understand what was going on inside. I learned there is a pattern[12] in how we try to deal with emotional wounding in our deeply individualized Western society. I had followed that pattern like a script, suffering inside while being a success in the eyes of the world.

Through my reading I learned how the health of the body is affected by unresolved trauma and ongoing stress. The immune system weakens and eventually collapses when the stress is too great for too long and physical illness, including "incurable" degenerative disease, is a predictable response to chronic stress.[13] I saw people around me who were examples of those effects. My intellectual understanding was at a high level—and my emotional pain was unrelieved.

I realized that two of the most important themes for my healing were shame and abandonment.[14] That understanding helped, but the pain still affected me in ways that were not visible to me.

It was then that I met Grant and learned EFT. While I had worked to heal physical and sexual shame for several years, using various modes of therapy, I found EFT to be more effective than anything else. Even so, the healing never seemed to be complete. As I gained experience as a practitioner of EFT, I understood that this was not due to the limitations of the technique; instead, the impediment was my inability or unwillingness to locate the deepest sources of my shame. It was when I began working with Grant that I found its origins.

Prior to beginning the research project, I did not understand that life in the womb could include trauma. I had no reason to think that pre-birth healing was needed or could be beneficial. In the research, however, it became clear that unresolved early traumas had been driving my worldview and behavior without me knowing it. I also discovered that some of these experiences were prenatal and some occurred after my birth.[15]

After experiencing the intense pain that every human must go through during pre-birth, I worked on healing that pain. Yet even with healing the traumas of my conception and birth, I still felt the pain of shame and abandonment so I realized that its origins must be somewhere other than in the developmental events I had already addressed and earlier than my childhood. There was only one place to go: back to gestation.

When I revisited my time in the womb, I gained a deeper understanding of the origin of my shame. *Since I was immersed in my mother's worldview and emotions while in the womb,* I had no other experience or reference points, so the thoughts, beliefs, emotions, and behaviors of her worldview became mine as well. As a consequence, I was born carrying my mother's shame, and I lived for years in an environment that reinforced and deepened that shame.

Arriving at this realization was not easy, and facing it was no fun at all. But the possibility of healing and liberation was exciting, and I approached it eagerly.

I applied a technique of regression I had developed in my EFT practice while working with clients whose issues were rooted in painful childhood experiences. Once in the womb, I used EFT to address my acquired shame and other issues arising from the womb environment. The process is described in more detail below.

I once worked with a client on a debilitating emotional issue. She suffered from a sense of personal worthlessness and a feeling of not deserving good things. She could not find its origin. I guided her into a meditative trance. Then I used the emotional content of her present-day feelings to provide a temporal conduit back through her life. She found memories from her teenage years, then her childhood. When I asked if she could go back further, she exclaimed, "Oh my god, I'm in the womb!" At that point she did not have a clear memory, but an impression, a feeling that was very real for her unborn self. We worked with that feeling using EFT. The emotional charge cleared. Then we came forward in time to later related memories, and addressed those as well.

The result was a complete healing, with no effects remaining in her current life.

It worked. As I felt the releasing and dissipation of my shame, I felt my mother's shame lifting and becoming lighter as well. Her shame was being healed at the same time! (It is a common occurrence in EFT practice for people who are close to each other to experience a resonance effect where the healing of one also benefits the other.)

In the course of this journey I have come to have much greater compassion for my mother. Her early life had not been easy, yet I know that beneath the pain, she loved me. It is sometimes not easy to see, but beneath whatever pain is present in their lives, our parents love us with a love that comes from their souls. Our essence is that we are manifestations of love both in our souls and in our humanness.

Three Steps to Healing

Negative beliefs, painful emotions, and other issues from pre-birth life are difficult to address. There are two reasons for this:

- First, what we experienced while in our mother's body was all we knew. To our fetal selves, the time in the womb was "normal," *regardless of what actually happened.* However, in meditation we can bring adult awareness and perspective to that time. When we do so, we see that what the fetus felt to be normal may not have been healthy at all. We can identify the painful aspects and traumas of that time.

- Second, this occurred before the age at which lasting memory develops. As a consequence it is inaccessible to our ordinary adult consciousness. Fortunately, it is not difficult to access clear perceptions of our pre-birth experience when we are in a deep meditative state or hypnotic trance.

For the fetus, and consequently for the baby, child, adolescent, and adult, both negative and positive aspects of the mother's life will always be present in deepest consciousness.[16] This can make the healing process challenging. The adult client and the healing practitioner must play detective to locate the pre-birth experiences that give rise to current issues.

Our human ego has a two-fold need: to understand and to be in control. Releasing the needs of the ego can be a considerable challenge for those of us who have found strength and safety in the power of our minds. It is fortunate that in deep meditation, our ego is left behind.

Here is the process I use to heal trauma or pain carried from times that are beyond the reach of normal memory. This process is effective with both emotional and physical issues.

1. We begin with careful questioning to identify the emotional content of the issue as it appears *today*.
2. Next I guide my client in a meditation of exploration. We use the mix of emotions identified in

the first step as a temporal conduit to move back to an earlier memory or impression with a similar emotional flavor. This may lead the client to an earlier time in this life, a time in the womb, or even a past life. Though there may be no obvious link between today's issue and the memory, there is no doubt that an important connection exists.

3. When we have revealed the source of the issue, we apply EFT. I will often also use other energetic or shamanic healing techniques. I bring to this work all the tools and guidance I have at my disposal.

Chapter 5: Compassion, Forgiveness, and the Journey of the Soul

The concepts in this chapter may contradict much of what you have understood to be true about life and death as it discusses reincarnation. If you find yourself resisting, I invite you to ask "What if it's true?" rather than dismissing what you read. If you suspend disbelief for a time, you may find that you are expanded and uplifted by the beauty and the possibilities of these discoveries.

The concept of reincarnation is not new. Diverse cultures have understood for thousands of years that we are a combination of an immortal soul and a mortal human body. Even in modern Western society, there is extensive anecdotal evidence for reincarnation.

This chapter presents potent support for the idea that we are both soul and human being. It discusses the work of a hypnotherapist who developed a process for guiding his clients to the realm to which our souls return after physical death. From the accounts of thousands of clients, he created a coherent model of what happens in that realm.

Linked to the journeys of our souls is the concept that not all conceptions result in perfect babies, and there is a great need for compassion and forgiveness.

The Journey of Our Souls

This section provides the needed context for understanding how fragile human life is in the beginning. Dr. Michael Newton began his career as a conventional hypnotherapist, if there is such a thing. Early in his practice he encountered two unusual clients. Their experiences while in hypnosis compelled him to expand his practice beyond the boundaries of a single lifetime.

The first client had a pain in his side that he couldn't heal until he went into a past life. The second client took Dr. Newton into a completely new area, an area which has traditionally been the domain of mystics and ancient spiritual traditions. It is the place of life between lives, where our human souls originate, and where we return to continue our learning between incarnations.

Over the next thirty years, Dr. Newton developed and applied a process which involved regressing the client into a past life. He would then guide the client through the last moments of that life, when the soul separates from the dying body and returns home.

In his first book, *Journey of Souls*, he presents a model of a typical time in the soul realm between incarnations. This model is based on the descriptions of more than 7,000 clients while they were in a deep trance.[17]

The first time I made this journey I was guided by a hypnotherapist trained at the Newton Institute. Since then, I have made the journey on my own a number of times. I use a combination of the techniques from the Newton Institute and what I have learned and applied on my own spiritual path.

The most profound aspect of every one of these journeys is that in that realm an inexpressibly beautiful and powerful love infuses every moment and every interaction. There is humor, even teasing, and directness combined with profound patience and understanding, but malice, power over another, and other negative or hurtful motivations and emotions are absent.

My first guided meditation to the realm of souls began with hypnotic regression to my most immediate past life. Then I moved through the death experience of that life and into the realm of souls. I was surprised by how easy the transition was, even though the death was violent. Toward the end of the three-hour session, I went to the place where I made plans for my incarnation in this current lifetime. I was attended by my guide, an advanced soul who has been with me from my beginning. In that place I experienced again the process of deciding on various aspects of this current life.

The greatest gift of that first journey was that I discovered my purposes in this lifetime, both as a soul and as a human being.

I also re-experienced preparing for my current life in cooperation with the souls who are now incarnated with me. During loving and patient discussions those other souls and I had with our guides, we designed the relationships and circumstances that would help us learn the lessons to which we had committed ourselves.

We all felt excitement and anticipation. We also knew that this was a time of serious consideration of our purposes for this incarnation. Together, we designed the family constellation into which we would be born, agreeing with each other on the major relationships we would experience and planning the general course of our lives. We decided what bodies we would inhabit (I chose my current one from among three).

In many cases, the souls with whom we incarnate in a family or in close friendships are members of our Soul Group, twelve to twenty souls who were created together. We know them well and have most likely incarnated with them many times before. (Have you ever had the feeling that you lived with someone in another life? There's good reason for that feeling: you did!) We work in partnership with them from one lifetime to another to determine who will be parents or children, and who will be siblings, other relatives, friends, and partners, and who may not be in that lifetime at all (as sometimes souls agree not to meet in that lifetime).

Does this sound too deterministic, too much like the plan? There is *a* plan, certainly; we created it ourselves before we came into our human body. Yet it is important to recognize that within the plans our souls made for this lifetime, we still possess free will. There are several stories in Dr. Newton's books from souls whose planned lives were altered in large or small ways by their (sometimes impulsive) exercise of free will during an incarnation. Sometimes the consequences were beneficial, and at other times they completely thwarted the plans those souls had made before they incarnated.

If you find resistance in yourself to the idea that you chose your family and your circumstances, you're in good company. When I first encountered this idea, I found it offensive. For years I refused to consider that it might be true. I didn't care for the situation and events of my childhood, and often felt that I should have had more compatible family members and companions. It was only when I made the journey into the place of life between lives that I saw my life in a much bigger context. I came to understand that the lessons I came here to learn are more important to the growth of my soul than I could comprehend from a human point of view.

Consider this analogy: Have you ever attended a weekend event or workshop that you knew would be difficult? It may have been challenging physically, emotionally, mentally, spiritually, or all these, but even with this foreknowledge you went, and you went willingly, because you knew from previous experience that you would learn and grow. From the point of view of the soul, a full human lifetime is like one of those weekends. You take on hardships to gain the benefits.

If you were born into a family or circumstances that were not pleasant, I invite you to examine the possibility that you chose that journey. You, as a soul, took on the challenge because it would assist you in your development. Many of Dr. Newton's clients, speaking from the realm of souls, told of previous lifetimes where they inflicted pain on other people. They then described how they decided to take on similar pain in this lifetime for their own growth and karmic resolution. Others told of receiving pain in one lifetime, then taking on the role of an abuser in a later life so they could understand the pain that drove the abuse. Through this experience, their soul was able to learn compassion for abusers.

I invite you to recognize that the souls that are in your children came together with your soul before you came into this life. You chose them to be your children, and they chose you to be their parents.

With this understanding, no parent and no child can possibly be unwanted.

This does not mean that the journey is easy. In fact, almost all lifetimes have difficulty in them (*almost* all—sometimes souls choose what is called a "reward life" after they have experienced a number of tough ones). We accept challenges because our souls know that there is a higher purpose in the hardship, pain, trauma, joy, love, and beauty in our lives on this planet. Souls also know that when they return home, there will be rejuvenation, acknowledgment, celebration, and limitless love for them there.

Incomplete Pregnancies and Perfectly Imperfect Babies

We live in a world where we are taught and even expected, in subtle and not-so-subtle ways, to blame ourselves when we are not perfect. With something as complex and uncertain as parenthood, it is easy to feel guilt or shame if we do not produce perfect children every time. What we *actually* need is compassion for all mothers, forgiveness for ourselves, and forgiveness for others. We also need the presence of human community to help us with the pain of what we perceive as loss.

We are far from perfect. In fact, more than two thirds of babies do not become healthy adults. Those of us who *have* attained healthy maturity are walking marvels!

In prenatal development, there are two situations that are potential sources of grief: incomplete pregnancies and the birth of a baby that is imperfect from the human point of view.

One of the first responsibilities of the mother's body is to determine whether a fertilized egg is capable of becoming a healthy baby. On physical and spiritual levels she must watch over that tiny being for the first several months after conception. If the time is not right, her body will end the pregnancy.

This happens much more than you might suppose. A review of research in the US concluded that "Based on the current evidence, if you factor in fertilized eggs that fail to implant along with pregnancies that end in miscarriage, around 70% to 75% of all conceptions will end in pregnancy loss."[18]

Premature births are another part of the picture. In 2016, about 10 percent of babies (400,000 in the United States) were born prematurely (before 37 weeks or 8.6 months).[19] Many of these babies do not survive the first day; others die within the first year, are disabled to some degree, or require long-term support.

What about the perfectly imperfect ones? In the US each year, approximately 3 percent of babies are born with what are called "birth defects."[20] In actual numbers, that is about 120,000 babies per year. In the UK, a government publication stated in 2018 that "Significant congenital anomalies affect between 2% and 3% of all births."[21] The March of Dimes organization stated in 2006 that "Every year, an estimated 7.9 million children—6 percent of total births worldwide—are born with a serious birth defect of genetic or partially genetic origin. . . . Hundreds of thousands more are born with serious birth defects of post-conception origin."[22]

I place quotation marks around the term "birth defects" because this experience takes on a transcendent meaning when we remember that the souls of the parents and the soul of a less-than-perfect baby have mutually chosen to have this experience for their own growth. There is nothing defective and much that is awe-inspiring about that.

Souls and Temporary Lives

Dr. Newton discovered that a soul will not merge with a human body before thirteen weeks after conception. The neurological development of the fetus is not sufficiently advanced. A soul may visit its human partner for "get acquainted" visits, but most souls do not fully enter into the relationship until the fetus is about twenty-one weeks old.

Dr. Newton spoke with many souls who partnered with babies who died before, at, or soon after birth. He found that the soul knows beforehand that the baby will not live. This is in accordance with the plan created in the realm of souls. In these cases, the soul often returns (also as planned) to join with the next baby conceived by those same parents.

Many of the souls who join with babies who will die young or be disabled are souls who have incarnated many times. They have progressed in their evolution to a point where they no longer need to incarnate. They have learned the lessons that having a body offers. Nevertheless, they take on this role willingly. They choose to be in a disabled body or mind, knowing beforehand the pain that both they and their families will endure. They make this choice from love, knowing that a less mature and less capable soul might be overwhelmed by the stresses of a short or difficult life.

Sometimes parents are aware that the body of their child with a disability is an ancient soul. I have a son who has lived beyond any expectations identified for him by his doctors. He has been epileptic since he was very young and has been wheelchair-bound for more than twenty years. Yet I know that his soul is very old, and I have met other parents who recognize ancient souls in their own disabled children. More of his story and my learning with him is found in appendix 4.

Chapter 6: A Method for Energetic and Spiritual Healing

This chapter describes the concept of meridian therapies, particularly EFT, for healing emotional and physical issues, including ones form before we were born. It discusses factors that can complicate the process.

The healing techniques known as meridian therapies have their origins in traditional Chinese medicine. As most people are now aware, the life-energy known as *chi* or *qi* flows in a network of pathways (meridians) within our bodies. If that flow is disrupted, the result is physical or emotional pain.

Dr. Roger Callahan discovered the connection between meridians and emotional distress in 1980. Since then, many methods using the concept of energy meridians have been developed to heal emotional issues. Acupuncture is the best-known meridian therapy as it has been used for thousands of years to address physical issues arising from a disruption in the flow of this energy. But there are several others, some developed more recently, including Emotional Freedom Techniques (EFT), Thought Field Therapy (TFT), neigong, BodyTalk, Tapas Acupressure Technique (TAT), and others.

It is now recognized that unresolved emotional pain causes many long-term physical issues (remember Gabor Maté, mentioned above). Now we also know that we can heal both physical and emotional suffering by dealing with the underlying emotional issues.

The method I have found most effective in my healing practice is EFT. The process of EFT is simple and rapid. It involves tapping on eight specific acupressure points on the body while visualizing or concentrating on an issue, negative memory, limiting belief, or physical pain.

Addressing a specific aspect often requires less than five minutes, and the effect is almost always immediate. Sometimes *complete* healing is nearly instantaneous, particularly when a single originating incident can be identified. Gary Craig, the originator of EFT,[23] calls these "One-Minute Wonders," and they are amazing and inspiring for both practitioner and client.[24]

Often there are other factors that require a more sophisticated approach. These factors can appear in the following situations:

- When many similar experiences reinforce the emotional impact of each other. An example of this is when PTSD is the cumulative effect of repeated trauma.

- When a painful experience creates a negative belief and later experiences are interpreted to reinforce that belief. For example, an early experience of separation can give rise to the belief that "People will abandon me." Later in life, any parting is interpreted as confirmation of that belief.
- When there is an invisible (to the client) payoff that is stronger than the desire to be free from the pain. An example of this payoff would be attention from caregivers or a strangely satisfying sense of victimhood.

Part of the good news of EFT is that you can do it on yourself, for yourself.[25] I have done EFT for myself with excellent results for more than twenty years. I sometimes say, only semi-jokingly, that I have tapped myself so much I should have calluses. I still tap today for a variety of reasons ranging from mild motion sickness to the residue of long-term emotional issues. Yes, my healing journey continues.

The process is easy. It can be learned even by young children. It is my wish that all children would learn in school to tap for themselves, and that the adults in their lives would learn that as well. If you are aware of your pain, you can be your own healer.

However, when we wish to heal effects that originated before birth, it can be challenging to find those origins. In this case the guidance and support of an experienced practitioner is beneficial. As a practitioner, I bring my objective point of view, my own spiritual guidance, and two decades of experience. I do not always do the tapping itself, as sometimes a client will do their own tapping, but I help the client "peel the onion": guiding the client—surprisingly easily—through layers of self-protection and the distractions of life to reveal and address what needs to be healed.

PART 4

A BRIGHT AND BEAUTIFUL FUTURE

This poem took sixty-five years to ripen and about an hour to put on paper. The healing of my prenatal traumas and environment were an essential part of that long process.

Forgiven

Would now that I could take in mine
the hands that left their
marks
on me

or quiet hear anew the words
that cut my heart and left
hard
scars.

If I could look into all eyes
that ever showed me
rage
or hate,

then
just to touch
to hear
to see
and love
would for me be
the greatest gift
I might this day bestow
or could this day receive.

Chapter 7: Beyond Healing: Welcoming the Anticipated Child

What if we know that a child is on the way? Can we escort that child through conception and growth within the womb?

This chapter discusses how we can accompany, guide, welcome, and love babies into our families at any point in their existence. We can be with the baby from the time of conception, or even before, from the time that the parents first establish their intention to create a new life.

The chapter looks at current methods that have been popularized for interacting with unborn babies. It then discusses the potential of deeper welcoming.

I invite parents to do their own healing so they can better understand and support the journey of their children.

Up to this point, I have focused on *retroactive* healing of pre-birth trauma. Clients for this healing are usually adults, and we deal with traumas from a time that is several decades in their past.

Healing pre-birth issues is straightforward for these clients. They enter a meditative state and apply the retroactive healing process discussed in chapter 5.

However, healing can also be done for babies who are still in the womb. This is accomplished using nonphysical communication to contact and guide that baby through the healing process.

The technique of retroactive healing in the womb sets the stage for an even more wonderful possibility. Imagine that we can greet, honor and accompany new children into our human community while they are still in the womb. Imagine that they can be born already knowing that they are welcomed, loved, and valued. Imagine that we can begin this *before they are conceived*. Imagine that when they are born, they meet the same people who greeted them as they came into existence and were with them as they grew within their mother!

Though it may seem radical to our society, this is not a new idea. Other cultures welcome children into existence before they are born. In *Women's Wisdom from the Heart of Africa*, Sobonfu Somé describes how every Dagara child is asked, while still in the womb,

> *"What are your unique gifts?" "What will you be born to contribute?" "What can your community do to assist you?"*

In *The Continuum Concept*, Jean Liedloff writes about a people in Venezuela whose interactions with their infants and children suggest they are welcomed before they are born, perhaps before they are conceived.

The San people of Africa have an understanding of their spiritual connections with one another that suggests they comprehend this as well. There are no doubt others. I hope so; we need their example, wisdom, and guidance.

A few years ago I was present at the birth of a baby boy. As labor became more intense and birth was imminent, I stepped back from the mother's bedside. I shifted into a deeper state of consciousness and contacted the baby. He was frightened, reminding me of my experience of that time. I acknowledged that the next short while was going to be difficult. I told him that I would stay with him, he would make it through, and he would be welcome in this world.

After the amazing moment of birth, I was invited to cut the umbilical cord. For a few seconds I pretended that I didn't quite know how to use a pair of scissors as I worked to assist the life force that remained in the placenta into his body.

I continued to send him messages of welcome and love until the post-birth protocols were completed. While he was weighed, I stayed close by, and he locked his eyes on mine. I knew that his eyesight would be unclear for several days, yet I felt that we were seeing each other. Then, as he was taken to his mother's breast and he turned his attention to her, I knew he was in good hands.

That baby now approaches adolescence. He is a wonderful child.

If you are more than twenty years old, it is unlikely that your parents understood the emotional significance of the pre-birth environment. This knowledge was not available. Now, we are aware of the potential of positive and loving communication between parents and their unborn child. Many websites and an ever-increasing number of books promote awareness and provide information for prospective parents.[26]

However, most of them only address physical ways of interacting with the fetus. They offer ideas about music, massage, or verbal expressions of love. But what if we could spiritually greet and go with the egg and the sperm that will become a new child? What if we could help the egg and sperm understand the magnificence of the dance of conception and prepare them for the difficult aspects of that event? What if we could accompany the embryo through gestation and birth? What if we could know *from the baby* what it was experiencing?

What if we could help it choose which aspects of its mother's life and beliefs it wished to retain and which it wished to transcend?

We can do all these things.

In earlier chapters, I described some painful experiences from my own prenatal life. I also described how healing transformed those experiences. My intention in telling these stories is to help you recognize the possibility and potential for healing your own pre-birth hurts. I believe that making the healing journeys that I have made will enable you to trust that you can bring forth healthy children. This is true even if your own early experiences were painful.

I have an invitation for prospective parents. If you are preparing to welcome a baby into this world, one of the greatest gifts you can offer your child is for *you* to be whole. Let that be your incentive to engage in your own healing.

As you revisit your time in the womb, you will gain appreciation for the intensity and potential impact of your pre-birth experiences. You will know how to welcome and guide your children because you know what they will encounter on *their* journey.

This is your birthright.

For Prospective Parents

Human intention is powerful. If you create the intention to communicate with your baby as a living, conscious being, you will be able to communicate with them *in both directions.*

I've been taught that when we are communicating with a spirit, the first thing we do is introduce ourselves. I suggest that you do this with your baby ("Hi, I'm your mom.") even if it seems completely unnecessary or even foolish.

Observe the response. You may be surprised how doing a simple greeting changes the nature and the power of the interaction!

Suspend disbelief. Be open. There will be lots of people around you who don't recognize that interactions like this are possible, and they will freely share their skepticism with you.

Give it a try. Treat it as an exercise in imagination, and *pay attention.* At some point you may have an experience that shakes and expands your view of what is possible.

You don't have to be able to go into a deep meditation—you likely don't have time for that anyway! But if you do have time, enter a meditative state and reach out to the baby. Alternatively, just have the intention to know what your baby needs. Imagine that your point of awareness is right there with the baby.

Hold in your mind the idea that the baby is capable of communicating with you. View your baby as a new, open, trusting life that needs your nurturing and protection.

Send love and reassurance, not only verbally but from your spirit, from your heart. The baby's heart begins to beat twenty-two days after conception, weeks earlier than the brain is significantly developed. You can communicate with the baby at the level of heart well before you can talk to them!

The electromagnetic field of an adult human heart is much stronger than that of the brain, at least sixty times stronger. It can be detected several feet away by measuring instruments. This scientific fact reminds me of a poetic quote from Blaise Pascal, a 17th century French mathematician, physicist, and theologian: "The heart has its reasons which reason knows nothing of ('que la raison ne connaît point') . . . We know the truth not only by reason, but by the heart." A surprising statement for a scientist—and true in ways we now comprehend better than ever as consciousness research continues to advance.

The heart quite literally has a mind of its own. It contains a sophisticated network of some 40,000 neurons known as the "heart brain." The heart brain can sense, feel, learn, and remember, sending messages to the head brain about how the body feels and more. Its strength is emotional intelligence, and its drive is to connect. Research has shown that the heart communicates information to the brain in several major ways and acts independently of the cranial brain.[27]

Ask your own body and the baby what they need. Pay attention to physical sensations and transient feelings in your body, particularly when there's no obvious reason for those sensations. This is the channel your baby uses to let you know about physical needs and wants.

Pay attention as well to transient and subtle emotions. If you sense distress, offer the baby reassurance and be curious and open about why the baby feels that way.

Since these sensations and feelings, both physical and emotional, may be very subtle, it may be necessary to find a peaceful environment to have these communications. Or they may be forceful and clear. That's the baby's developing personality showing up!

I invite you to contact me if you would like to have assistance or coaching in communicating with your baby. Keep an eye on the events page at www.windwalker.ca as well. There you will find training workshops on topics related to this book and others.

Chapter 8: Conclusion

As you can see, there is potential for stress, trauma, and injury to our yet-to-be-born selves. But we can use EFT to reveal and heal the traumatic aspects of that experience.

Healing is available to every parent and every child. We do not need to carry pain, guilt, shame, loneliness, or any other negative residue (the list is long) from our parents' experiences or our own.

I have seen the power of this healing for myself and my clients. Other researchers, parents, therapists, and witnesses also have stories about the benefits of pre-birth healing.

We don't have to wait for a whole new generation before we can see the impact of this healing. We can heal our own pain from before birth, and we can feel different today. In so doing we become instruments of the healing and evolution of all of human life, and through that, all life on this beautiful planet.

It is our birthright to be whole. One time as we were preparing to enter a sweatlodge ceremony, my Anicinabe teacher said, as though stating an obvious truth, "The Creator intended for us to have good lives."

The time to do *your* healing is now. It is never too late. The only need is willingness to pursue your own healing. This willingness arises effortlessly when you believe in your right to have a good life.

We can also apply these techniques for those yet to be born. We can interact with our children through their earliest moments, days, and months, and be present with them in beautiful and supportive ways, helping them to heal as needed and guiding them through the journey of life before birth.

These practices have the potential to give us children who are born emotionally and psychologically healthy. They will arrive in the world unencumbered by the stressful events and environmental challenges of the womb. From the beginning they will know the world as a beautiful, supportive, healthy community. They will be with each other and this entire world in an atmosphere of mutual love and respect.

They will be born whole.

Appendix 1: A Life-Changing Vision

This is the story of an experience I had several years before I met Grant McFetridge. The vision I was given that night put me on the path that prepared me to work with him.

I emerged from the darkness and heat of the sweat-lodge, "the womb of our mother, the Earth," into a moonlit night in July. For a moment, my mind engaged in considering whether to go and bathe in the nearby river as we had been invited to do, or find a place that would allow me to be in reflective solitude. But before I could move, I was pulled as though by an invisible rope to a chicory plant at the edge of the clearing. (It was the same chicory plant I had used for target practice with a primitive weapon two days ago.)

I found myself on my knees in front of the chicory. My hands went effortlessly into the soil around its roots and awareness of my physical surroundings disappeared. The spirit of chicory, the one who had called me to herself, commanded my full attention. She directed my awareness to other plants in the wild hedge beside the corn field, then to the hardwood forest on the hill on the other side of the field.

She said, "I speak for us all. Know us. Know that we are one with you. You need us, and we need you."

There was much more than these words can convey: a loving connection accompanied by an invitation, an opportunity, an imperative. The communication felt like a summons to a commitment.

I had no idea how long I was on my knees, unaware of my surroundings or the movement of other people. When I came back to physical awareness, I was alone. During the time that I had been with the chicory, forty more people had emerged from the sweatlodge and disappeared into the night. How long was that? I did not know. It felt like seconds, but it must have been many minutes.

Hearing voices and laughter from the river, I walked toward the sound. But before I arrived at the river, I found myself turning left, down a dead end trail. A burdock plant taller than me said, "Do not go to the river. Pay attention to what the chicory told you."

There was nothing more to do. I went to bed.

I had never entered sleep so quickly or slept so deeply. When I came awake, I was in the same position as when I lay down: on my belly, face to the right, arms limp at my sides.

I knew that I must go outside.

There was enough light to see, but the sun was not yet up. How long had I slept? One hour? Four hours? It was well after dark when I went to bed, and dawn came early at that time of year.

I walked out into the cornfield that surrounded the teaching area. There was a small clearing where the corn was stunted. I had been called here for a reason, to be given the next step after my encounter with the chicory. Overwhelmed with emotion, tears flowing on my face, I lifted my face up and asked what I was to learn.

My eyes were closed. I was surrounded by a dark sky, feeling as though I had been transported somewhere far from the cornfield. Across the darkness, in bright silver script, I saw the word "patience." With that word came a message of affirmation and reassurance.

There was more. I was told that I would need to be patient. I understood also that I was to learn and hold a vision of spiritual connection with the natural world. This connection would require me to know all beings in the world around us both spiritually and physically. I was to work with those other beings and with my human relatives in service of the beauty, mutual commitment and possibility for wholeness that we share.

I was to bring this vision to the people I was teaching and to many others, in ways I could not yet conceive of. I would need to do this with the patience that deep learning and a deep transformation require, both for me and for those whose lives I would touch.

This would be the work of a lifetime, perhaps many lifetimes.

I returned to my bed and slept soundly until the call came to rise for breakfast.

Appendix 2: Four Days Without Water

This is the story of a powerful experience of solitude in nature, and some of the lessons I learned in that time and place.

André looked at me and said, "What are you taking with you?"

"Sleeping bag, under pad, tarp and ropes in case it rains, my ceremonial materials, and some water."

"No, you're not."

"Huh? Not what?"

"No water."

I gaped at him, stunned. *Four days without water?!?*

This was to be my third Vision Quest: four days and nights of solitude in a wild place, looking within myself, asking the universe and the spirits of the natural world for guidance and insight about the direction of my life.

Having been taught and guided by wise and competent elders, I was confident that I would be able to explore my questions without being distracted by physical hardship. Until I met André.

I had decided to do this Quest alone, and I told a friend, Christiane, of my plan. A few days later, she called me—she had someone she wanted me to meet, a medicine man named André.

The three of us talked about the Vision Quest. I told them the date I would leave.

The day of separation came. As the sun came up, I went down to the sweatlodge and prepared the fire. While the rocks heated toward glowing red, I sat facing the fire and pondered the next few days. It felt good to be alone.

I heard a call. I looked up, surprised, to see Christiane and André coming down the hill. Christiane greeted me, then moved away. André sat beside me on the log. I began to talk about something inconsequential. He stared at me, expressionless, until I stopped, then he said, "There's something you need to do."

It was a perfect setup. I had not asked him to guide me on this Vision Quest. He was now letting me know, in a way that I could not refuse, that he was there to do just that.

I returned to my house and brought back a pouch of tobacco. I asked him formally, according to the protocols I had been taught, to guide me on my Quest.

He accepted the tobacco, and with it my request. Then he told me I was to go without water.

I was frightened. I had fasted for four days on previous Vision Quests, but had never gone without water. In my wilderness first aid training, one advanced instructor had said that tissue damage begins after twenty-four hours without water. I had decided that "tissue damage" was not something I cared to experience. So, of course, I would take water. Now André was telling me no.

I had a choice to make. I could refuse his guidance and go alone, or I could face one of my biggest fears, suffering and dying helplessly and pointlessly. My hours and days alone in the wilderness, my ancient survival skills training, my previous fasts—none of that prepared me for this. This was unknown territory.

I would be alone. There would be no one to ask for assistance, and it would be a long walk to get help. My only contact with the human world would be five sticks that I had laid on the ground out of sight of my Quest location. Every morning I would stand one of them upright in the ground to indicate that I was okay. Someone would come every day to check that a new stick was standing.

Somewhere within, I knew that I needed to face this fear. André waited while I came to my decision. Now, I do not doubt he was praying for me to find the highest course.

A few minutes later, we dumped out the six gallons of water I had put aside.

That decision, that act, changed the whole Quest.

After the sweatlodge ceremony, André drove me to the drop-off point. He walked with me to an old barbed-wire fence about ten minutes from my circle. My threshold. He turned away in silence, and my time of solitude began. I crossed the fence, noticing for the first time the bear hair caught in the wire, and walked to my circle on the trail made by that bear.

I spent the rest of that first day settling in: preparing a sleeping spot, rigging my tarp under a big cedar tree, completing the ring of stones that marked my circle, and getting to know the area within the circle.

Seeing the bear's trail crossing my circle, I honored the spirit of bear and asked this one to allow me to be in its home for the next four nights. As darkness fell, I went to bed.

When I awoke next morning, I had no feeling of being on a sacred Quest: I felt no anticipation, no sense of connection, no purpose. It felt like a bad camping trip, where I had forgotten my tent, food, equipment, water, matches, and books. What I had with me was barely enough to prevent me from dying of hypothermia.

I could not find the reason why I was here. I had made a big mistake.

All I could think to do was say, as I had done nearly every morning for years, "Thanks for the day"—a small ceremony of gratitude for the gift of one more day of life. When I spoke those words, I felt no gratitude, only numbness and an undercurrent of despair. I heard the words in my head, but that was all.

Then, as I finished speaking that simple sentence, everything transformed. I felt no hunger or thirst, no fatigue, discomfort, or confusion. I saw the beauty and meaning in everything around me and in my own life. I became present to the experience of the Quest.

For the next four days I was with Spirit.

I had chosen my circle area beside a pond, making the circle big enough that one edge of it was in the water. Early on the third day, after a light rain, I went down to a small willow that stood with its feet in the pond. The tip of one of its long lance-shaped leaves curled up slightly and held a single drop of sparkling clear water. I stood for a long time with that beautiful drop of water, admiring it, loving it, immersing myself in the awareness of how vital water is to all life. I knew that I would not touch that drop, even as I imagined its brilliant coolness caressing my tongue.

Sometime during that day, I learned to draw the essence of water into my body from the pond.

There were other lessons and gifts offered to me as well. One of them was a new ceremony of healing for my sweatlodge—a gift to be brought to my people. Other experiences from that time are not to be written, only spoken, and then carefully. Some are not to be told at all.

When André appeared to bring me out on the morning of the fifth day, I had no sensation or symptoms of dehydration.

I came back renewed. I brought with me new gratitude, gifts, understandings, power, and a sense of the possibilities of my life and my path. All of this was made possible by accepting the challenge to step up, to face the unknown.

Christiane and André, *migwetch*—thank you.

Appendix 3: The Beginnings of Physical Existence

Later in the research, Grant and I decided to take another journey. This was a side trip from our initial pre-conception-to-birth itinerary. We would begin again at the point when the Chosen One among the eggs was about to be released from the ovary. However, this time we would move not forward but *backward* in time. Our goal was to investigate what occurs before the proteins, genetic material, and other components come together to create the wondrous complexity of a human egg.

The journey backward in time was fascinating but uneventful. I observed how self-aware I the egg was before being released from the ovary, then I (adult observer) watched myself (egg) go into a state of dormancy as we moved backward together along the timeline. Once again I felt like the audience at a play where I was also the performer.

As the egg became dormant and lost its sense of individuality, I no longer felt personally identified with it. Moving earlier in time, I came to the point when that egg was coming into being in the body of a female fetus (*my* mother) within the womb of *her* mother, some twenty-seven years before I was conceived. The component physical parts of the egg disassembled as I watched, like a movie in reverse, until there was nothing left that I could identify as the egg. Yet there was still an "I" observing, and this pure awareness continued to move backward.

Then, a surprise, as I transitioned from physical being into *nonbeing*. I passed from the realm of physical existence into another realm. This place was unlike anywhere I had been in previous meditative journeys.

I was surrounded by a luminous velvety blackness with no boundaries. I had no body, none of the density or heaviness of physical existence, only intelligent awareness. I could move, expand, and observe in all directions at once. Though I was unaware of any other features or beings, I sensed that this space was not empty.

I could not perceive boundaries in any direction, and as far as I could extend my awareness on this first visit, I was alone. In later visits I met entities there who were like the space itself: large, diffuse, gentle, and loving of all physical reality.

I became aware of a wavelike movement from my "left," which oddly felt like east. I felt the sensation of floating in a warm ocean, being lifted and lowered by long swells on an otherwise unruffled surface. I stayed in that place for a time, trying to reach far enough to detect the origin of the swells. I was unable to do so.

In my next journey to this realm, I discovered the nature of those waves. They are pulses of energy full of unmanifested potential. When that potential condenses, when the wave function collapses (to use an image from quantum mechanics), it results in the physical reality that we experience every day. It is those waves that energize the assembly of atoms, molecules, amino acids, and other more complex matter into biological life. The quality of their energy is *creative intention.*

After making these discoveries, we turned our attention back to the time after conception. Both Grant and I were fascinated by what we had found, but we did not explore this realm further at that time. We had discovered that trauma in the mother before the egg is released from the ovary is unlikely to have significant effects on a baby. That was enough for the purposes of our research project.

Appendix 4: The Story of My Son

I have a son. I've never played catch with him. I didn't help him learn to ride a bicycle. I've never taken him fishing. I've never gotten on his case about getting better grades in school, or showed him how to change a tire, or talked to him about what it means to be a man.

When he was just over one year old, something went awry in his development. Over the next six months, he declined into epilepsy and autism, and almost lost the ability to walk. He never did develop the ability to express himself with words.

My ideas about what it would mean to be an ordinary father to an ordinary son never had a chance.

If by now you're feeling sorry, don't. He has taught me more about the emotional richness of being a man than anyone else in my life.

One of the first things I learned about from him was love. I learned that I am capable of loving unconditionally and love can bring with it immense pain. I learned how it feels to be helpless to protect someone I love.

I also learned about courage: his, mine, my family's. My son in particular amazed me with his courage. Early on, when he was around the age of two, staying on his feet was a struggle. He was having fifty or more seizures a day, and though they were not all grand mal seizures, he would often fall when a seizure came.

Electroencephalographs showed a continuous electrical storm in his brain. For him to stay upright in that state demonstrated immense courage and tenacity. He still demonstrates that same courage even as he is confined to a wheelchair.

He also taught me about my capacity to experience pain and continue to function. At that time, it was important for me to be able to set pain aside when I needed to. I did not learn to be grateful for that pain until many years later.

I learned about my capacities for both tenderness and callousness. I learned about my anger, and that underneath that anger was fear and a strong sense of unfairness. I learned how to channel my anger into good work, and how beneficial physical activity could be as a release.

I have learned to accept his path as well as my own. One of the greatest gifts of my experience with him is that I now, finally, recognize that I have felt and will continue to feel genuinely, intensely, and deeply. I have also learned that to be a whole man, I need to do more than acknowledge and face my emotions. I must also explore, claim, and teach from them.

In my relationships and work, the lessons that I have been given through my son have enriched and empowered what I now offer to the world.

Appendix 5: Skepticism and Validity at the Frontiers of Knowledge

It is important that we recognize that babies experience awareness before birth and even before conception.

We're not there yet. The impediment has been that accounts of pre-birth awareness and experience have not been considered valid. Investigation of life before birth has been beyond the reach of the scientific methodology that insists that if it can't be measured, it doesn't exist.

Ken Wilber addresses those who dismiss the validity of exploration of realms of higher awareness through meditation:

> *If you're skeptical, that's a healthy attitude, and we invite you to find out for yourself, and perform this interior experiment with us, and get the data, and help us interpret it. But if you won't perform the experiment, please don't ridicule those who do.*[28]

Part of the message of this book is an invitation to "perform this interior experiment" in the time before we are born.

In order for the results of an experiment to be valid, they must be reproducible and consistent. When the results of anecdotal or subjective research meet this criterion, we can make sound conclusions. An excellent example of this is Dr. Michael Newton's research into the life of souls in the time between incarnations. He constructed a detailed map of the realm of souls based on his work with more than 7,000 hypnotherapy clients. His work has been confirmed and extended by many other hypnotherapists and their clients. These descriptions are valid because they are both consistent and reproducible.

Until recently, few psychologists believed in or investigated prenatal or perinatal trauma. Nearly ninety years ago, in the early years of psychology, Austrian Otto Rank offered the novel idea that there might be such a thing as birth trauma.[29] In 1974, Dr. David B. Chamberlain began using hypnotherapy to discover and resolve traumas arising in the womb and at birth.[30] He has written about the consciousness of babies in the womb.

Dr. Stanislav Grof has developed a model called prenatal matrices that describes the phases of labor and birth, the traumas associated with those phases, and the effects of those traumas in later life.[31]

Dr. William R. Emerson has studied both pre- and perinatal psychology and has developed methods to identify and heal wounds originating in the prenatal and perinatal periods.

Sheila Fabricant Linn, Dennis Linn, and Matthew Linn, who have worked with Dr. Emerson, have written about their personal experiences with prenatal spiritual healing.[32] They work within a Christian paradigm, and are inclusive of other approaches as well. Their book provides a different and often beautiful perspective. The events they describe are similar to what I experienced.

Nancy Hearn, Dr. Joye Bennett, and Elizabeth Clare Prophet also offer insights and exercises for welcoming and guiding babies on this journey.[33]

Today, there is an increasing number of books and internet resources that refer to or describe prebirth experience. The Association for Prenatal and Perinatal Psychology and Health[34] brings together people from a variety of professions interested in this field.

Until recently many psychologists and doctors have viewed prenatal experience as beyond reach or not significant. This reminds me of beliefs from psychology and medicine that assumed infants below a certain age did not even *feel* pain, or that if they did, they forgot the experience and it had no lasting effects. In 1975 I was told this directly, in an incident involving my own infant son.

This is changing. Few medical practitioners would support those ideas today, and many agree that prenatal experience is highly significant.

The kinds of tools and experiences described in this book and the other resources mentioned above will become commonly used for research and therapy. Techniques for studying the time in the womb will continue to be developed and refined.

This area is fertile ground for more investigation. The potential for alleviating pain and the potential for growth are immense.

Further work in this area will contribute both to the growing up of our species as we evolve socially and psychologically, and to the waking up of our spiritual selves.

How You Can Work With Me

1. **Windwalker Healing: services for pre-birth trauma or other life issues**
   - Private Emotional Freedom Techniques and energetic/shamanic sessions in person, by phone, or online to heal pre-birth (or past life, or current life) traumas and issues.
2. **Windwalker Spirit Workshops: training in spiritual awareness, expansion, and power**
   - A series of experiential workshops where you create a personal connection with spirit, nature, and yourself and learn to bring the power and beauty of your spiritual path into every day and every action.
3. **Born Whole Parenting Training: communicating with your unborn child**
   - An intensive workshop where you learn how to enter a deep meditative state and be in communication with your child on the journey of growth in the womb.

4. **Guided journey to the realm of souls**
   - Discover the awe-inspiring beauty, love, and power of the realm of souls. Meet your guide and your soul group, the souls of the people who are important in your current life. Learn about the purpose of this lifetime and the purposes of your soul.
5. **Group training in your region**
   - Arrange a group training session in your region for any of the topics discussed above. You will work to bring together others in your locale who are interested in this work as a group or who wish to have individual sessions.

Check out www.windwalker.ca to see what calls to you.

Interested? Want more information? You can reach me directly through my website, or by email at wgietz@windwalker.ca.

Acknowledgments

Number One: Monica, who pushed, encouraged, and loved me through the process of realizing that I had a story worth telling, writing the story, seeing its deeper meaning, and staying with it all the way to publishing. You believed in me when I didn't. Without you this book would not exist.

To Grant McFetridge, who recruited me to be Guinea Pig #2 and directed me to places I would never have gone without your conviction and determination.

To the people who reviewed early crude versions of the book and offered honest and kind suggestions for improving it: Michael Bergob, Bob Blaxley and Brenda Naylor, Dr. William Emerson, Kelly Farley, and Grant again. Also in this group are the many who listened to me talk about the topic and encouraged me to believe that it is an important contribution, particularly Ian Byington, who made the adventure enjoyable with your stories and guidance. To Jessica Fan for your work to make the back cover a good vehicle for my message.

Volunteer proofreaders, for your keen eyes and your encouragement: Jill Banting, Andrew Baskin, Alexis Kiselyk, Alyssa Kohlmann, Laura Jesson Love, Corinna Stevenson, and Charlotte Watson.

About the Author

Wes Gietz's life has spanned a variety of disciplines and worldviews. These days he identifies himself primarily as a writer. He is also a teacher of spirituality and awakening, a guide of life advancement through coaching, and a practitioner of energy healing techniques. He is qualified as an Integral Associate Coach®.

His formal education includes Bachelor's degrees in Chemistry/Mathematics and English Literature, and Master's degrees in Biochemistry and Public Administration. He gained 20 years of experience in training, strategic planning, and human resource management in corporate settings and as a consultant. He has taught business communication, statistics, and human resource management at the University of Victoria and North Island College.

He has studied with Tom Brown Jr. and Jon Young, and has been guided by the writings of David R. Hawkins, Michael Newton, and Ken Wilber.

He has practiced natural skills and beliefs for over fifty years, including ancient skills of survival and living, spiritual awareness and philosophy, the ceremonies of daily life, and the ceremonies and responsibilities of the sweatlodge. He is acknowledged as a storyteller, a shaman, an elder, a leader of ceremony, and a person who demonstrates the qualities of patience, wisdom, compassion, and understanding.

He has done the Vision Quest four times, and guided Rites of Passage for individuals and groups for 20 years. He has taught a nature-based path of spiritual awakening and power for 25 years. In 1999 he initiated the Firemaker Primitive Skills Gathering, an annual week-long learning and celebration of ancient skills and community.

He has applied and taught Emotional Freedom Techniques to healing present-life, pre-birth, and past-life trauma for over 20 years. EFT has been a powerful part of his own healing journey.

Prior to writing *Born Whole*, he published numerous articles in various journals and newsletters on topics such as edible and medicinal plants, spirituality, healing, tracking, and Coyote Mentoring. He is a contributing author of *Peak States of Consciousness, Volume 2: Acquiring Extraordinary Spiritual and Shamanic States* (Grant McFetridge with Wes Gietz). He has been engaged as a public speaker on many of these same topics.

Thanks for reading my book!

Would you help me improve this book and make future books better?

Please leave a review on Amazon; rate the book and tell the world how this book touched you.

Mention this book to your friends and social contacts.

Thanks so much! You're helping make this beautiful world more beautiful.

Endnotes

1 William R. Emerson, "The Vulnerable Prenate," *Journal of Prenatal and Perinatal Psychology and Health* 10, no. 3 (March 19, 1996). An excellent summary of this article and a list of reference works is provided by Peter K. Gerlach at http://sfhelp.org/gwc/news/prenate.htm; Peter W. Nathanielsz, *Life in the Womb: The Origin of Health and Disease* (Ithaca, NY: Promethean Press, 1999).

2 Tom Brown Jr's Tracker School is at https://www.trackerschool.com/.

3 One of my most important early reads was Tom Brown's book entitled *Grandfather* about the life of his teacher, Stalking Wolf.

4 See Appendix 5.

5 For a more detailed discussion, see https://brainworksneurotherapy.com/what-are-brainwaves.

6 There are exceptions: think of a woman who struggles with alcohol or drug dependency, or a girl who experiences ongoing trauma and whose system is constantly flooded with cortisol and worse. These can affect the development of the egg.

7 Joseph Chilton Pearce discusses this state in *The Biology of Transcendence: A Blueprint of the Human Spirit* (Rochester, Vermont: Inner Traditions International, 2002)

He describes it in the context of adolescence, a feeling within young people that something big and wonderful is about to happen in their lives.

8 I refer to the sperm as "he" because the sperm feels masculine regardless of whether its genes are male or female. Similarly, when I refer to the egg, I use the pronoun "she."

9 Adapted from http://www.gaiatheory.org/overview/

10 I express my deep gratitude to Grant for making available to me the recordings and transcriptions from our work together.

11 Scott Peck. *The Road Less Traveled* (New York: Simon and Schuster, 1978),75-76

12 This range of responses is interestingly similar to the stages of dealing with the prospect of death described by Dr. Elizabeth Kübler-Ross in her ground-breaking book *On Death and Dying* (1969).

13 See Gabor Maté *When the Body Says No* (2003) for an insightful and compassionate exposition of this process from a well-researched medical point of view.

14 In my work with Emotional Freedom Techniques I had come to believe that abandonment is a nearly inevitable consequence of our growth. It is certainly one of the most common wounds that shows up as my clients and I "peel the onion." I now understand feelings of abandonment as an overreaction to the normal process of healthy individuation. This perspective makes healing much easier.

15 This book addresses the time before birth, in this lifetime. Two related topics are generational or epigenetic pain (pain carried from our ancestors) and

pain acquired after birth. These are topics outside this discussion. All of this pain is real. It can be addressed using the same process that is described in chapter 6 for healing of prenatal hurts.

16 Let it be clear that the stressful experiences of the womb do not always lead to pain or dysfunction later in life. One impressive aspect of human beings is how much stress we can experience without significant debilitating effects. We are resilient and we are strong.

17 I use the terms "trance" and "meditative state" interchangeably. Both of them involve changes in the frequency of brain waves, generally into the Theta or Delta level.

18 Krissi Danielsson, *"What Do Miscarriage Statistics Really Mean?"* Verywell Family, https://www.verywellfamily.com/making-sense-of-miscarriage-statistics-2371721.

19 "Preterm Birth | Maternal and Infant Health | Reproductive Health | CDC," Centers for Disease Control and Prevention, https://www.cdc.gov/reproductive-health/maternalinfanthealth/pretermbirth.htm.

20 "Data & Statistics on Birth Defects | CDC," Centers for Disease Control and Prevention, https://www.cdc.gov/ncbddd/birthdefects/data.html.

21 Martin Ward-Platt, "The Work We Are Doing on Birth Defects," Public Health Matters, 2019, https://publichealthmatters.blog.gov.uk/2018/03/03/the-work-we-are-doing-on-birth-defects/.

22 https://www.marchofdimes.org/materials/global-report-on-birth-defects-the-hidden-toll-of-dying-and-disabled-children-wall-chart.pdf

[23] Gary's website is www.emofree.com. There is an excellent overview of EFT at https://www.emofree.com/eft-tutorial/tapping-basics/what-is-eft.html in his website.

[24] One of my most powerful and rewarding experiences with EFT was a ten-minute healing of Virginia's long-standing and debilitating endometriosis. You can read that story at http://windwalker.ca/efttapping/emotional-freedom-techniques-in-action/

[25] See https://www.youtube.com/watch?v=XWoad-Q8WIYA for a teaching demonstration of the EFT process.

[26] An excellent bibliography is found at https://birth-psychology.com/content/birth-psychology-bibliography-2000-2015 in the website of The Association For Prenatal And Perinatal Psychology And Health.

[27] HeartMath LLC and HeartMath LLC, "Let Your Heart Talk To Your Brain," HuffPost, December 07, 2017, https://www.huffpost.com/entry/heart-wisdom_b_2615857.

[28] Ken Wilber and Lana Wachowski. *A Brief History of Everything*. (Boulder, CO: Shambhala Publications, 2017).

[29] A good biography is found at https://en.wikipedia.org/wiki/Otto_Rank

[30] Dr. Chamberlain's website is http://www.dbchamberlainphd.com/

[31] Dr. Grof's website is http://www.stanislavgrof.com/

32 Sheila Fabricant Linn, *Healing Our Beginning,* Amazon, July 01, 2005, https://www.amazon.com/Healing-Beginning-Sheila-Fabricant-Linn/dp/0809143305.

33 Elizabeth Clare. Prophet et al., *Nurturing Your Baby's Soul: A Spiritual Guide for Expectant Parents* (México: Patria, 2010).

34 The APPPAH website is https://birthpsychology.com/.

Made in the USA
San Bernardino, CA
30 January 2020

63580866R00090